CHANGE THE STORY,
CHANGE THE
FUTURE

OTHER BOOKS BY DAVID C. KORTEN

Planned Change in a Traditional Society
Bureaucracy and the Poor
People-Centered Development
Community Management
Getting to the 21st Century
When Corporations Rule the World
Globalizing Civil Society
The Post-Corporate World
The Great Turning
Agenda for a New Economy

DAVID C. KORTEN

NEW ECONOMY WORKING GROUP

CHANGE THE STORY, CHANGE THE FUTURE

A LIVING ECONOMY FOR A LIVING EARTH

A Report to the Club of Rome

BK

Berrett–Koehler Publishers, Inc.
www.bkconnection.com

Berrett-Koehler Publishers, Inc.
1333 Broadway, Suite 1000
Oakland, CA 94612-1921
Tel: (510) 817-2277 | Fax: (510) 817-2278 | www.bkconnection.com

ORDERING INFORMATION
Quantity sales. Special discounts are available on quantity purchases by corporations, associations, and others. For details, contact the "Special Sales Department" at the Berrett-Koehler address above.
Individual sales. Berrett-Koehler publications are available through most bookstores. They can also be ordered directly from Berrett-Koehler: Tel: (800) 929-2929; Fax: (802) 864-7626; www.bkconnection.com.
Orders for college textbook/course adoption use. Please contact Berrett-Koehler: Tel: (800) 929-2929; Fax: (802) 864-7626.
Orders by US trade bookstores and wholesalers. Please contact Ingram Publisher Services, Tel: (800) 509-4887; Fax: (800) 838-1149; E-mail: customer.service@ ingrampublisherservices.com; or visit www.ingram publisherservices.com/Ordering for details about electronic ordering.

Berrett-Koehler and the BK logo are registered trademarks of Berrett-Koehler Publishers, Inc.

Printed in Canada

Berrett-Koehler books are printed on long-lasting acid-free paper. When it is available, we choose paper that has been manufactured by environmentally responsible processes. These may include using trees grown in sustainable forests, incorporating recycled paper, minimizing chlorine in bleaching, or recycling the energy produced at the paper mill.

Library of Congress Cataloging-in-Publication Data

Korten, David C.
    Change the story, change the future : a living economy for a living earth / David C. Korten.—First Edition.
        pages cm
    "A report to the Club of Rome."
    Includes bibliographical references and index.
    ISBN 978-1-62656-290-5 (pbk.)
    1. Human ecology—Religious aspects.   2. Economics—Religious aspects.
3. Ecotheology.   I. Title.
GF80.K665   2015
304.2—dc23   2014037720

First Edition

20 19 18 17 16 15 | 10 9 8 7 6 5 4 3 2 1

Produced and designed by BookMatters, edited by Karen Seriguchi, proofed by Janet Blake, indexed by Leonard Rosenbaum, and cover designed by Wes Youssi, M80 Design

Dedicated to
Thomas Berry, who inspired my search for a new story

Living Earth, the source of our birth and nurture

and

My granddaughters, Rhiannon and Allegra
May theirs be a Sacred Life and Living Earth future

CONTENTS

No problem can be solved from the same
level of consciousness that created it.

—ALBERT EINSTEIN

For peoples, generally, their story of the universe
and the human role in the universe is their primary
source of intelligibility and value. The deepest crises
experienced by any society are those moments of
change when the story becomes inadequate for
meeting the survival demands of a present situation.

—THOMAS BERRY, *The Dream of the Earth*

Let ours be a time remembered for the
awakening of a new reverence for life.

—THE EARTH CHARTER

FOREWORD

The Club of Rome is proud to have David Korten as one of
its members. He is outspoken. Not all people like that. We
do, not least because of the dire state of the world. A con-
tinuation of current trends—both in social and ecological
terms—will inevitably lead to collapse. This is also David
Korten's core message. Not exactly a new message for the
Club of Rome.

What is new in David Korten's approach is the emphasis
on the "Story" that will be needed to move society toward
sustainability. In his words: *When we get our story wrong,
we get our future wrong.* He describes the dominant story of
the global economy as a Sacred Money and Markets story in
which money is humanity's defining value, an unregulated
global market serves as its moral compass, and destroying
life to make money counts as wealth creation.

At a deeper level, David explores the implications of
three basic cosmologies—our stories of the origin, development structure, and meaning of the universe. He iden-
tifies three cosmologies that are instrumental in our time:
The "Distant Patriarch" cosmology of the monotheistic

religions, Judaism, Christianity, and Islam; the "Grand Machine" story of a mechanistic universe that denies purpose and meaning; and the "Mystical Unity" cosmology in which we are all connected by the timeless eternal One.

Grounded predominantly in the Grand Machine cosmology, the Sacred Money and Markets story supports a global society characterized by selfishness, the absence of meaning, a strong belief in markets, and a concentration of institutional power. David makes the case for a Sacred Life and Living Earth economic story grounded in a Living Universe cosmology in which each human being is an intelligent, self-directing participant in a conscious, interconnected self-organizing cosmos on a journey of self-discovery toward ever greater complexity, beauty, awareness, and possibility.

Surely, this gets us into mystical and esoteric domains. This is not the usual thinking at the Club of Rome. But we acknowledge the strength in David's reasoning that the old stories have not led us toward a desired future but ever deeper into the mess we are in. We welcome fresh thinking. And we welcome the author's search for meaning and purpose and for realistic strategies confronting the prevailing destructive forces seen in the Sacred Money and Markets story.

We very much welcome initiatives that try to change the paradigms of the present economy, such as the New Economy Working Group, which has been initiated by David Korten and colleagues. It is an informal, US-based alliance of organizations and individuals coordinated by the Institute for Policy Studies. It is dedicated to articulating and popularizing a bold vision and implementing a strategy for a New Economy that works for all people and the living systems on which their well-being depends.

We recognize, of course, that huge controversies will result from a book questioning the wisdom of free trade agreements, calling business leaders generously compensated servants of money-seeking corporate robots, and suggesting that the money economy is a "suicide economy." Not all Members of the Club of Rome will have the same view on the topics. After all, David Korten's book is a report *to* the Club of Rome, not a formalized credo *of* the Club of Rome. But we at the Club of Rome feel united in the belief that business-as-usual strategies are no longer possible in a physically limited world nearing nine billion people with growing expectations for ever higher consumption—a world where, in addition, income disparities are growing and the risks for social exclusion are considerable, not least among unemployed youth.

We welcome the discussion on David Korten's basic tenet that the wrong story will lead to the wrong future, and that a better story is very much needed. His proposal for a new narrative—a Sacred Life and Living Earth story grounded in a Living Universe cosmology—is provocative but a most welcome contribution to the debate.

We invite readers and commentators to turn to us at www.clubofrome.org.

September 2014
Ernst von Weizsäcker
and Anders Wijkman,
Co-Presidents, The Club of Rome

CHANGE THE STORY,
CHANGE THE FUTURE

Choice-making beings of many possibilities, we humans live by shared cultural stories. They are the lens through which we view reality. They shape what we most value as a society and the institutions by which we structure power.

When we get our story wrong, we get our future wrong.

We are in terminal crisis because we have our defining story badly wrong. Seduced by a fabricated Sacred Money and Markets story, we live in indentured service to money-seeking corporate robots and relate to Earth as if it were a dead rock for sale.

Communications technologies now give us the capacity as a species to choose our common story with conscious intention. This is a moment of unprecedented opportunity to create a future consistent with our true nature and possibility as living beings born of a Living Earth born of a Living Universe.

An authentic Sacred Life and Living Earth story is emerging. It has ancient roots in indigenous wisdom. If embraced, it changes everything.

Change the story, change the future.

PROLOGUE

IN SEARCH OF A DEEPER TRUTH

Some twenty years ago, while writing *When Corporations Rule the World*, I often made the case in public presentations that we humans are on a path to self-extinction. I was startled by responses like "I agree. It does seem like we are on a suicidal course. But the changes you are talking about are impossibly big and costly. And the dismal projections may turn out to be wrong."

It seemed that many thoughtful people were saying, "We can't change. So let's party while we can. If it ends, it ends. Last one to leave, turn out the lights." I wondered, does life have so little meaning that people are not willing to make an effort to change even if their children's future and species' survival are at stake?

While wrestling with this question, I read Thomas Berry's *Dream of the Earth*. I sensed a profound truth in his argument that our future depends on finding a story that gives us a powerful reason to live—a story that answers the basic question: Why?

I've since come to realize that such a story must accomplish four things: It must give life meaning and purpose. It must give us reason to believe that the necessary changes are possible despite powerful opposition. It must address the claim that we are by nature individualistic, greedy, and competitive. Finally, it must point the way to a viable human future.

I find hope in the many shifts that have already occurred. Most everyone I meet recognizes that change is essential and the barriers are enormous. Many wonder whether it is too late. Hardly anyone in my acquaintance now suggests it is not worth the effort to try.

In the pages that follow, I share the results of my search of the past twenty years for a story that reflects the breadth of human knowledge and understanding and provides a guide to action that meets the needs of our time. This prologue is the story of personal experiences that drew me to the search and gave rise to critical insights.

WAKING TO THE WONDER OF THE WORLD'S RICHLY VARIED CULTURES

In my youth, I had no concept of cultural diversity and assumed I would spend my life in the monocultural white American middle-class Protestant town where I was born.

The most exotic person with whom I had a direct relationship was my Catholic aunt with red hair. She was very sweet and I loved her, but the Catholic thing and the red hair seemed a bit strange to my young mind.

Nothing in my life from birth through all but the final months of my undergraduate college experience even hinted at the possibility I might spend twenty-one years of my adult life living and working in Ethiopia, Nicaragua, the Philippines, and Indonesia deeply immersed in the extraordinary diversity of the world's peoples, cultures, and religions. Likewise, it was beyond my comprehension that during my adulthood the barriers of geography would melt away as technology connected the world in a seamless web of instantaneous and nearly costless communication.

During the course of my life experience, I became acutely aware of how the shared culture of a people serves as a lens that shapes the perceptions and behavior of its members in ways both beneficial and destructive. This awareness led me to appreciate the immense range of our human stories and possibilities, the potentially devastating consequences of getting our story wrong, and the benefits of getting it right.

DEAD-WORLD ECONOMICS ON A LIVING EARTH

People commonly refer to me as an economist because I speak and write about the economy. The label makes me deeply uncomfortable.

I started out as an economics major in college. After three courses, however, I concluded that what my economics professors were teaching had little practical relevance. I switched to psychology and, in graduate school, focused on organizational system design—how institutional structures shape our collective behavior.

I've since come to realize that most academic disciplines, even those that claim to be strictly objective, operate within a particular story frame—a shared cultural lens. That lens serves to discipline the discipline. Like any cultural lens, however, it can be self-limiting. Economics is a prime example.

A colleague recently suggested that, viewed through the cultural lens of mainstream economics, Earth looks like a dead rock populated by mindless money-seeking robots. The choice of this lens by the economists who teach our college students and shape our public policy perhaps explains my intuition and decision to switch to psychology. It also helps explain why many economists celebrate rule by corporations that act like money-seeking robots seemingly intent on turning Living Earth into a dead rock in disregard of the needs of living people and nature.

FROM HOMETOWN TO GLOBAL COMMUNITY

During my undergraduate years at Stanford, I was extremely conservative and greatly concerned about the threat that communist revolutions posed to our American way of life. This concern led me to sign up for a senior colloquium on modern revolutions. There I learned that the revolutions of the twentieth century were largely a response to the frustrations of poverty.

I decided to devote my adult life to bringing lessons of Western business success and the comforts of our consumer culture to the poor of the world's "underdeveloped" countries. I believed that if they became "developed" like us, they would forget the revolution nonsense. That belief shaped my life for many years.

More Praise for *Change the Story, Change the Future*

"*Change the Story, Change the Future* will transform your view of reality and human purpose. One of the most important books of our time, from one of the most brilliant thinkers of our era, it hands us the keys to a world in which all people live in creative, peaceful, and coproductive partnership with one another and with nature. Read it, ponder its message, and spread the word!"
—**Thom Hartmann, progressive internationally syndicated talk show host and bestselling author**

"David Korten truly is a visionary. In this book he answers the question, why is our world so destructive of people, place, and planet? *Change the Story, Change the Future* is a profound telling of how our current political economy is guided by a cultural story that is leading us in a deadly direction. Drawing on the latest science, the insights of indigenous wisdom, and his own remarkable life, Korten brings forth a new story that affirms our lives as participants in living communities."
—**James Gustave Speth, founder and former President, World Resources Institute; cofounder, Natural Resources Defense Council; and author of *Angels by the River***

"This slender volume offers a radical rethinking of how we might frame a positive story to lead our species out of its current impasse. The result is a book that is genuinely optimistic but not naive—a remarkable feat."
—**Denis Hayes, organizer of the first Earth Day; President, Bullitt Foundation; and author of *Cowed***

"Joining the wisdom of the great spiritual teachers with findings from the leading edge of science, *Change the Story, Change the Future* outlines a transformative new narrative that is both promising and powerful. Read this book, reflect on the implications, and help bring a new story to the fore of public consciousness."
—**Van Jones, founder and President, Rebuild the Dream, and author of *Rebuild the Dream***

"*Change the Story, Change the Future* is one of the most thought-provoking analyses of the shifts in Western ideals and modern society now available under one cover. It provides a new template for thinking about God, the world, and our own immersion in what we call 'the mind of God.'"
—**Sister Joan Chittister, OSB, Executive Director, Benetvision, and author of *A Passion for Life***

"David outlines a fundamental truth in this powerful and groundbreaking new book: changing the way we view our role on the planet is the first and most crucial step toward a truly regenerative future. For those ready, this book will become a new source of clarity—it will shatter all notions holding us back from true progress."
—**Jason F. McLennan, CEO, International Living Future Institute**

"David Korten's brilliance shines through in his understanding that to save Earth, ourselves, and democracy, we must change the story that governs how we understand the world and our choices. It is a truth both simple and profound. He delivers a compelling new story to guide our transition from a corporate-power to a people-power future."
—**John Cavanagh, Director, Institute for Policy Studies, and Cochair, New Economy Working Group**

"Once you read this book, you'll never be able to look at today's tired old stories the same. Read it and then join the growing movement that is creating new stories—stories that guide us toward the better future we know is possible. Let's go!"
—**Annie Leonard, Executive Director, Greenpeace USA, and author of** *The Story of Stuff*

"If ever there was a guide to a better future, this is it. David Korten's life journey has brought him (and now us through this book) to a profound understanding of the need for a life-enhancing story to guide us forward. Thank you, David!"
—**Maude Barlow, National Chairperson, Council of Canadians; 2005 Right Livelihood Award winner; and author of** *Blue Future*

"This small pebble of a book is an act of immense generosity. After a lifetime of reaching for the root causes of our malaise, David Korten has unearthed a simple truth: the story that enslaves us is not the real story. Read this to remember that our true nature is to be a good neighbor on a nurturing, competent planet."
—**Janine Benyus, partner and cofounder, Biomimicry Institute, and author of** *Biomimicry*

"David Korten tells a beautiful story about the power of story. We create the world according to the stories we tell ourselves; what power there is in this one realization. This gem of a book calls us to examine our core assumptions about how the world works so that we can cocreate a new, evidenced-based story that is alive with possibility."
—**Frances Moore Lappé, author of** *EcoMind*

"Human exploitation of God's creation and the resulting consequences, such as climate change, are threatening all that God calls us to care about. In his accessible, insightful, and provocative new book, David Korten masterfully explains the pernicious worldview that got us to this point and suggests a new paradigm that we will need to adopt if we wish to preserve the Earth for future generations. Anyone who cares about the future of our planet and our human family should read this book."
—**Jim Wallis, President, Sojourners; Editor-in-Chief,** *Sojourners* **magazine; and** *New York Times* **bestselling author of** *The (Un)Common Good*

"Another way—a truth aligned with what it actually is to be human—is emerging as an organizing principle for this era: interdependence. New science has shown that the essence of humanity is in fact to be connected to each other, to our purpose, and to the natural world. David Korten speaks the truth in this book—and it is the path to peace and deep joy."
—**Michelle Long, Executive Director, Business Alliance for Local Living Economies**

"*Change the Story, Change the Future* is tremendous. David Korten has written *Common Sense* for our time. This book will put our feet on solid ground so we can move steadily and wisely into the future with the natural world as our partner."
—**Peter Buffett, Copresident, NoVo Foundation; musician/composer; and author of the** *New York Times* **bestseller** *Life Is What You Make It*

"David Korten has written a 'mythos beyond modernity' that opens the mind to a new way of being in a world newly seen in which we are coparticipants in a knowing, acting (perhaps at the quantum variable level upward), participatory, coevolving living universe."
—**Stuart Kauffman, affiliate faculty, Institute for Systems Biology; Emeritus Professor of Biochemistry, University of Pennsylvania; and author of** *Reinventing the Sacred* **and** *At Home in the Universe*

Gradually, I came to realize that the reigning story—that economic development brings forth a world of universal prosperity—is deeply flawed. The reality I experienced was far different. The more the GDP grew, the more brutal life became for the majority of people, the faster environmental devastation spread, and the faster Western media-driven cultures of individualistic violence, greed, and consumer excess displaced once-rich living cultures.

Eventually I realized to my horror that these same destructive trends were playing out in my home country—the United States—and in all the other countries we look to as models of development achievement.

As I dug further, I came to see a near-universal pattern. Economies were growing financially at the expense of life. Development brought a few individuals more money and more life. Most individuals, however, got a bit more money and a lot less life. The consequences were clearly visible for people at the bottom, for whom the net consequence was less food, less access to clean water, less basic security, and less joy.

On reflection, I came to see the connection between the story lens of economics and business education, and the social and environmental devastation I was witnessing. Public policies shaped by that lens were shifting power from people and nations to global corporations and financial markets delinked from moral sensibility and public accountability. With time, my search for insights into the source of this delinking reawakened a long-suspended spiritual search that had begun much earlier in my life.

FROM RELIGIOUS AFFILIATION TO SPIRITUAL QUEST

Growing up, I participated actively in our local nondenominational Protestant Community Church. I was scarcely aware of the variety of the world's religions and took no interest in them.

Then, as an undergraduate at Stanford, I took a course in comparative religion. A remarkable professor opened my mind to the commonalities of the world's religions and to the parochialism characteristic of competing religious traditions.

After finishing my MBA in 1961, I spent a summer in Indonesia. While traveling by train through Java's spectacular terraced rice fields tended by humans working in harmony with the land as they had for countless generations, I experienced a profound sense of the interconnection of humans and nature in a circular flow of time. I became enthralled by the beauty, insight, and wonder of traditional Indonesian culture and life in harmonious co-productive partnership with nature.

It was the first step in my awakening to the significance of how deeply our cultural lenses shape our values, our perceptions of and relationships to one another and to Earth, and our sense of meaning and purpose.

On my return home, I gave a slideshow presentation on my Indonesian experience to a group of my parents' friends. The gathering included the pastor of a local church, who asked me, "What religion do the Indonesians practice?" I said, "Islam." He responded, "That's too bad." "Why?" I asked. "Because," he said, "Islam is an ethical monotheistic religion. That makes Muslims difficult to convert to Christianity."

I later asked myself, "If ethical monotheism is supposed to be the highest religious expression and Islam is an ethical monotheistic religion, why should we want to convert Muslims to Christianity? Is it only about market share?" I have never since been inclined to affiliate with a particular religious denomination.

THE STEP BEYOND DEAD-WORLD SCIENCE

My introduction to the importance of our choice of basic cosmology—our story of the origin, development, structure, and meaning of the universe—began in October 1962, when I was a doctoral student at the Stanford Business School. My wife, Fran, told me about a university-wide graduate seminar on human consciousness offered by Willis Harman. We decided to take it together.

Harman, at the time a professor of electrical engineering, was one of several prestigious Stanford scientists who openly asserted that the reductionist, mechanistic assumptions and methods of science had become self-limiting. Harman had a particular interest in the relationship between matter and consciousness. Does consciousness manifest from matter? Or does matter manifest from consciousness? His working hypothesis was that they are inseparably intertwined.

This encounter with a brilliant teacher with impeccable scientific credentials who dared to challenge the prevailing intellectual orthodoxy of science in search of the deepest truths was a life-changing, intellectually liberating experience. Harman remained a friend and intellectual mentor until his death in 1997.

MONEY AGAINST LIFE

I entered a career in international development with a very idealistic view of America's role in the world as a selfless defender of democracy and benefactor of the poor. While serving abroad I had the opportunity to observe the global expansion of corporate power from the perspective of those who experienced firsthand the resulting cultural, economic, and political corruption.

One of my most powerful insights into the mythic illusions driving development's dysfunctions came during a ten-day retreat in November 1992 in Baguio, a mountain resort in the Philippines, with the leaders of several of Asia's most influential nongovernmental organizations (NGOs). All were Asian except for me. It was an unstructured reflection on the Asian development experience and its implications for Asian NGOs seeking to end poverty.

We had all worked together over a number of years and had become aware that the "Asian development miracle" much touted by the World Bank and free market economists was both limited and superficial. Beyond the dynamic competitive economies of South Korea, Taiwan, Hong Kong, and Singapore was the deeper reality of impoverishment and environmental disruption spreading across the region. We spoke of economic development as a process of monetizing relationships that had once been based on a sense of mutual caring and obligation between people, and between people and the land.[1]

One evening as we gathered after dinner to continue the discussion, an image came to mind of development as a pool of money spreading across the Asian countryside, consuming life wherever it touched. It was reminiscent of *The Blob*, a horror movie in which a transparent, featureless mass of protoplasm engulfs humans and animals in its wake, dissolving and absorbing their flesh.

In the case of development in Asia, it was as if money itself had become a purposeful evil force, absorbing intelligent and highly defined living beings to grow its own featureless bulk—money consuming life to grow money.

I puzzled for months over that image. What exactly is money that it might act with a seemingly willful drive to consume life? As I reflected on this question, I realized that money is just a number created by humans, with no meaning outside the human mind. That it might be an independent, self-directing force in its own right made no sense. Yet the consequences of money's growing reach were becoming so real and so clear.

Then I realized that the only possible source of the willful drive in this evil scenario is our own human will. The only motivating force is the misdirected life energy of human society.

It took me rather longer to realize that this misdirection is the consequence of an illusion: that money is wealth and the measure of our individual and societal worth. Focused on money, rather than on the life we really want, we yield the power and will of our life energy to institutions structured to seek financial gain by any means.

What we call development is a process of alienating people from the lands and waters from which they make their living. They then become dependent on money to obtain essentials like food, water, shelter, and energy. That makes them dependent on the institutions that control their access to jobs and credit—the means of acquiring money.

Eventually I realized it is the same for all societies, including my own. As our dependence on money replaces our direct relationships with one another and nature, we turn to money as the measure of our accomplishment and relinquish control of our lives to institutions that control our access to it. We have an economy designed to make money for rich people. We need an economy designed to support everyone in making a living.

STORY POWER

Fran and I moved from Manila to New York City in 1992 to share what we had learned about the nature and causes of, and the alternatives to, the development failure that we had witnessed. It would also be an opportunity to study and address what we were coming to recognize as the source of the problem we had gone abroad to solve.

As soon as we settled in New York, I began writing what would become *When Corporations Rule the World*. That, in turn, led to my connection with a small and extraordinary group of international activists who came together as the International Forum on Globalization (IFG) and birthed the global people-power resistance against corporate globalization. I learned from that experience the extent to which power flows to those who control the framing stories of global society.

Prior to 1995, corporate interests largely controlled the story on trade agreements and a globalizing economy. In their version of the story, trade agreements eliminate economic borders to bring the world's people together on a path to universal peace, prosperity, and democracy.

The IFG provided a forum through which our small group shared stories of the devastation wrought by corporate-led economic globalization. Together, we developed the reality-based counterstory that global corporations use trade agreements to make an end run around democracy to consolidate global corporate rule. Many people recognized the truth of this counterstory, and a global resistance movement was born. In the United States, that movement burst into public consciousness with the historic 1999 Seattle WTO protest. From that experience, I gained tremendous respect for the power of citizen movements galvanized by an authentic story.

The defining struggle of our time is a contest between corporate power and people power. It is a struggle between money and life as our defining value and between plutocracy and democracy as our system of governance.

Corporate power aligns with the interests of money. The

expanding people-power movement aligns with the interests of life. Corporate power mobilizes around a well-defined Sacred Money and Markets story spread by corporate media and a corporate-dominated educational system.

The people-power movement mobilizes around a wide variety of peace, justice, and sustainability initiatives. It yet lacks a recognizable unifying story of sufficient power, clarity, and visibility to successfully challenge the story that legitimizes corporate rule. To prevail, people power needs its own story.

TELL ME YOUR IMAGE OF GOD

In the fall of 1999, I spoke at Global Economic Justice, a conference organized by the Washington State Association of Churches and the Church Council of Greater Seattle. It was a lead-up to the Seattle WTO confrontation. I shared the podium with Marcus Borg, a respected academic theologian and New Testament scholar. The defining statement of Borg's presentation reached deep into my consciousness: "Tell me your image of God, and I will tell you your politics."

Borg explained that the image of God as a distant patriarch translates into a hierarchy of righteousness and supports a politics of authority, domination, and competition for power. The image of God as a universal spirit manifest in all creation supports a politics of cooperation, compassion, and sharing. He noted that both images find strong support in the Christian Bible.[2]

Borg's linking of image and politics was a reminder that

our defining stories have serious implications for the societies we create. I recognized for the first time how the image of God as a distant patriarch might serve to support and legitimate a concentration of power in imperial corporations and governments deeply at odds with the teachings of Jesus and other great religious teachers.

The image of a universal spirit manifesting as what we experience as material reality points to the interconnection of all beings and to the possibility of deeply democratic societies. It is also the foundation of the Living Universe cosmology and the Sacred Life and Living Earth story outlined in the pages ahead.

SACRED EARTH MOTHER

Much later, in March 2012, I was a guest at a small gathering of indigenous environmental leaders convened to discuss the then-upcoming debates of the Rio+20 UN Conference on Sustainable Development.[3] These leaders observed that in preparatory meetings, Wall Street interests proposed that to save nature we must value her, and to value her we must price her.

This worldview pointed to a familiar pattern: First price, then privatize, then commodify, and finally securitize. Within the framework of the global market game, the Wall Street proposal would give those with the most money a license to further monopolize and exploit at will, for their private gain, the gifts of nature essential to human life—all in the name of protecting nature.

A defining moment came at the end of a brief presentation by Karma Tshiteem, secretary of the Bhutan Gross National Happiness Commission. He summed up with three words, "Time is life." Those words have since been at the fore of my consciousness as an expression of the extreme contrast with the ruling Western axiom, "Time is money."

I found myself strongly aligned with the indigenous story that Earth is our Sacred Mother. Her care is a sacred responsibility of all humanity. She is beyond price and not for sale. The profound significance of this insight reached deep into my mind and heart. It did not feel sentimental. It felt like the essential and pragmatic foundation of a viable human future.

The deeper I go in my exploration of the cause of the human crisis, the more I come to believe that our human hope for the future requires that we recognize and honor Earth as a living being, the source of our birth and nurture, our Sacred Mother.

A GRAND SYNTHESIS

Three months after the gathering of the indigenous leaders, I joined a meeting convened by the Club of Rome in Bristol, England. Its purpose was to plan an initiative to engage a global discussion of the values that shape our common future. At that meeting, I shared simple versions of what I'm calling the Distant Patriarch, Grand Machine, and Living Universe cosmologies and how each of these characterizes reality. I also shared my thoughts about their implications for how we have chosen to organize as a global society.

Martin Palmer, who hosted the meeting, asked me whether these cosmologies are mutually exclusive. My instant response was, "Yes, of course." As I later reflected on his question, I came to doubt my response. I recalled the Hindu story of six blind men describing an elephant, each insisting that the part they were touching was the whole elephant. Perhaps each of the cosmologies I had outlined described an element of a larger and more complex reality.

I pulled my thoughts together in a short essay and circulated it among participants in the Bristol meeting and a few other friends and colleagues. The enthusiastic and insightful responses motivated me to develop the essay further.

Early versions of the essay became the focus of conferences in Washington, DC, and New York City organized by the Contemplative Alliance. These conversations prompted further revision. I added what I here call the Mystical Unity cosmology and named and outlined the prevailing Sacred Money and Markets and the emerging Sacred Life and Living Earth stories.[4]

Note that I use the term *Living Earth* in two ways: as "a Living Earth" (a living entity) and as "Living Earth" (a proper name).

THIS BOOK

In January 2014, I shared the essay with Jeevan Sivasubramaniam at Berrett-Koehler Publishers, who shared it with Steve Piersanti, B-K's president and publisher and my guide on each of my previous trade books. They suggested I develop the essay into a short, accessible book for people who need no proof that we humans are on a bad path, who are well aware that a global economy driven by soulless financial markets and corporations threatens our common future, and who are looking for a coherent and practical articulation of the truth in their hearts.

Change the Story, Change the Future is a summation of the insights of a lifetime of dramatically varied experiences. It touches on pretty much everything. To keep it short posed a significant challenge. Of necessity, it limits the elaboration of nuances and the documentation of conclusions. I reference only a few favorite sources in the endnotes.

Some reviewers noted their unease with references to spirit and the sacred and suggested eliminating them to make the book acceptable to a broader audience. I appreciate their honesty and intention, but they have missed my central point.

We humans live by our shared framing stories and have a deep need for a sense of purpose and meaning. If we do not share an authentic sacred story, the void will be filled with an inauthentic story—and that is our problem. An economy, a society, built on the foundation of a lie cannot work.

I urge those so wounded by their experience with formal religion that they are inclined to dismiss any work that suggests a spiritual perspective to bear with me and consider the possibility that a frame for understanding the deeper mysteries of our existence may be relevant to our future.

Others have noted that my initial descriptions of the classic cosmologies do not take into account the intellectual ferment currently under way that touches on science, religion, and every other field of human thought. That ferment is a major source of my hope for the future and shapes the chapters ahead. My intention in this book is to demonstrate the depth and significance of the contrast between the story by which we currently live and the nature and implications of the story now emerging. We start with the former.

1 OUR STORY PROBLEM

Economists debate how to accelerate economic growth. Scientists debate how long the human species can withstand an economy that is destroying Earth's capacity to support life. Social activists debate how to reduce an intolerable and growing gap between the profligate and the desperate.

Meanwhile, corporations compete for monopoly control of the information commons and what remains of Earth's freshwater, fertile soils, minerals, and fossil fuel. The growing demand of energy-intensive economies for fossil fuel drives environmentally destructive extraction methods like fracking, deep-sea drilling, and mountaintop removal. Competition for food and freshwater increases in the face of population growth; extreme drought and flooding; the conversion, destruction, and depletion of farmland; and the contamination of freshwater sources.

Politicians dependent on big money to fund their campaigns advance policies that favor the interests of money over the interests of life. Economists ease the conscience of those politicians with assurances that such policies accelerate growth in the gross domestic product, which in turn will end poverty and fund technologies to eliminate our human dependence on nature.

Money prospers. Life withers. We cannot eat, drink, or breathe money. No matter how fat our bank accounts or advanced our technologies, we depend on Earth's health for food, freshwater, clean air, and a stable climate.

Some among a confused and desperate public respond to the contradictions with denial. Some look for ways to profit financially from the devastation. Some pray for divine intervention.

Our hope lies with the growing millions who work to heal our human relationships with one another and nature in a bold effort to turn the human course. Through thought and deed, they are authoring a new story of meaning and possibility. It is a story with ancient roots and profound implications for our economic relationships.

THE ESSENTIAL ROLE OF A SACRED STORY

Many indigenous people use the term *sacred* to refer to what is most important, most essential to the well-being of the community and its members, and therefore most worthy of special respect and care. It is in that sense that I speak here of sacred stories.

We humans live by stories. A shared story is the basis of the ability of any people to live together as an organized society. A society's ability to organize as a secure and prosperous community depends on the authenticity (validity) of its story. Authentic stories are generally the product of the shared experience of a people and take form through largely unconscious processes extending over generations.

There are also inauthentic sacred stories fabricated to serve the interests of a ruling class at the expense of the rest. We currently organize as a global society by such a story, and we bear the tragic consequences.

SACRED MONEY AND MARKETS

While preparing dinner each day, I listen to the evening edition of NPR's *Marketplace*. Its focus is money. Two questions dominate: Is the GDP growing, how fast is it growing, and why? Did major stock indexes rise or fall, and why?

Every day on every consequential news outlet, similar programs focus our attention on how the financial economy is doing. Any mention of how people and nature are doing is usually in the context of assessing the implications for the GDP and stock prices—financial indicators that speak to how money and the moneyed are doing. To listen to the discussion, you would infer that the purpose of people and nature is to serve money.

These reports have a consistent familiar frame. I call it our Sacred Money and Markets story. It goes like this:

Time is money. Money is wealth. Material consumption is the path to happiness. Making money creates wealth, drives consumption to increase happiness, and is the defining purpose of individuals, business, and the economy.

Those who make money are society's wealth creators.

Affluent lifestyles are their fair and just reward for their contribution. Poverty is a consequence of laziness.

Humans are by nature individualistic competitors. That is a blessing, because freed from distorting regulation, the invisible hand of the free market channels the individual and corporate drive for profit to choices that maximize economic growth and thereby the wealth and well-being of all.

Just as a person's income is a measure of their worth and contribution to society, so too the profit of the corporation is the measure of its worth and contribution. As a legal entity that aggregates talents and interests to increase the economic efficiency of the individuals within it, the corporation is properly considered to be a person in its own right and entitled to the same rights as any other person.

As corporations create wealth, governments consume it. The functions of government should be limited to assuring the common defense, securing property rights, and enforcing contracts.

Economic inequality and environmental damage are a regrettable but necessary and unavoidable cost of growing the GDP. GDP growth in turn eliminates poverty, drives technological innovation to free us from our dependence on nature, and brings universal and perpetual prosperity for all. There is no viable alternative to a profit-driven free market economy.

Economics courses in our most prestigious institutions teach this story as settled science. The corporate media constantly repeat it. Over time, money has become contemporary society's object of worship. Making money has become life's purpose, shopping a civic duty, markets our moral compass, institutions of finance our temples, and economists the priests who provide absolution for our personal and collective sins against life. Pope Francis correctly named it idolatry—idol worship.

Thoughtful readers will readily recognize—or at least suspect—that every assertion of this Sacred Money and Markets story is false or grossly misleading. The story is based on bad ethics, bad science, and bad economics. We now see the environmental devastation, economic desperation, social alienation, and moral and political corruption this fatally flawed story leaves everywhere in its path.

Profit itself is not the problem. A modest profit is essential to the health and survival of any private enterprise. Managing the economy to maximize profit for the benefit of a financial oligarchy is, however, a recipe for economic, social, and environmental disaster—as America's experiment with unrestrained greed dramatically demonstrates.

WHEN MONEY-SEEKING ROBOTS RULE THE WORLD

A favorite science fiction plot portrays robots that turn rogue and become a threat to their human masters. Unfortunately, that plot isn't a fictional future; it is a current reality.

In the 2012 US presidential election, Republican candidate Mitt Romney famously declared that corporations are people. Apparently, he hadn't noticed the distinction between the corporation as a self-governing legal entity and the living people in its employ. The demonstrated inability of US Supreme Court justices to recognize the distinction gives new meaning to the phrase "Justice is blind."

People are living beings. We have bodies. We eat, breathe, love, and reproduce. We live in community and exercise moral conscience and sensibility in our relationship with our living neighbors. We bear legal responsibility for our crimes and our harms against others. We die.

A corporation has no physical body, conscience, or moral sensibility. It has no need for air, food, or water. It does not love, reproduce sexually, or have a natural life span. It has no fear of imprisonment or execution for its crimes.

The only consequential thing that a corporation has in common with a living human person is the legal doctrine that grants it some of the same rights enjoyed by natural persons—but without the corresponding responsibilities.

Publicly traded corporations are legally protected pools of money-seeking financial assets. They take no notice of collateral damage to life. The living people in their employ, including CEOs, are paid employees required to leave their personal values at the door and subject to dismissal without recourse at the corporation's pleasure.

The corporation's primary accountability is to global financial markets driven by human traders and high-speed supercomputers engaged in gaming market prices for quick profits with no concern for long-term value. The financial institutions (corporations) for which these traders and computers work are the ultimate money-seeking corporate robots. They have well-documented histories of deception and criminality in the pursuit of unearned profits. They favor financial speculation over real investment, encourage and reward fraud, drive continuing cycles of economic boom and bust, mire people and governments in debt they cannot pay, and hold national governments hostage to the interests of global financiers.

If these corporations were just the people they employ, then most of the world's global bankers would be in prison.

Titular human owners—such as the beneficiaries of a retirement fund—rarely have any direct involvement or say in the affairs of the corporations they "own." Whatever their involvement, they are as owners explicitly exempt from civil or criminal penalty for the corporation's crimes.

Under this system, the Money Economy prospers. Its corporate robots use their profits to buy up the rights to ever more of Earth's living wealth. A privileged few among those who serve the robots enjoy lavish rewards. Those not in the inner circle of privilege struggle to survive job losses, declining real compensation, growing debt, and increasing competition for what remains of the living wealth on which their lives depend.

Economists point to growth in GDP and financial assets and assure us that society is getting richer. They take no note that Earth's living wealth, the real wealth on which life depends, is in accelerating decline.

In recent decades, the corporate robots and their extravagantly compensated minions have expanded their control of the institutions of media, education, and politics to construct a shared public story. Lulled into a trance by the constant assurances that money and shopping are the keys to our health and happiness, we submitted to corporate rule.

For so long as we leave it to money-seeking robots to shape our shared story and economic priorities, they determine our shared future.[1]

GLOBAL AWAKENING

The gap between the Money Economy story and the Living Economy reality of people and nature is growing so extreme and obvious that the Sacred Money and Markets story is losing its grip on the public mind. People are reawakening to our nature as living beings born of a Living Earth born of a Living Universe. As we reawaken to our true nature, we see more easily that the Money Economy is a numbers game driven by self-directing corporate robots for which life is nothing more than a tradable commodity. That game would be irrelevant except for the resulting increase in unearned financial assets—and thereby the economic and political power of the winning robots.

We are eroding Earth's capacity to support human life. Growth in human population and individual consumption intensifies competition for what remains of Earth's declining real wealth. The corporations with excess financial assets buy up the remaining capacity in order to extract monopoly profits from the humans whose lives depend on access to that capacity. The greater the financial returns to the corporate robots and the few they favor, the greater their ability to expand their monopoly control to extract more profits and further increase their relative share of economic and political power. Earth dies. Human suffering spreads. Public and private institutions lose their credibility, the social fabric frays, and the global system becomes increasingly unstable.

To many of us, these consequences come as no surprise. The spiraling system collapse is playing out much as forecast by the computer models described in *The Limits to Growth*, the highly controversial study by the MIT Systems Dynamics Lab published in 1972 as a report to the Club of Rome.[2] The future is here.

Guided by a Sacred Money and Markets story, we have created a global suicide economy designed to make money with no concern for the consequences for life. If our goal is short-term growth of the financial assets of a tiny financial oligarchy, then the system is a brilliant success.

Most efforts to avoid further collapse focus on treating the symptoms of a system failure with marginal adjustments: a new regulation, a tax on bad behavior, a subsidy incentive for good behavior. Such adjustments might be appropriate if we were dealing with a broken system. When dealing with a self-destructive system supported by a false story, the only solution is a different system grounded in a different story.

Fortunately, the elements of a new story are emerging. These elements are the cultural equivalents of the imaginal discs that guide the caterpillar's transformation from larva to butterfly. The more quickly and clearly we give expression to the new story, the more rapidly we may find our way to a just and sustainable human future.

SACRED LIFE AND LIVING EARTH

Here are some defining elements of the emerging story. I call it the Sacred Life and Living Earth story.

We humans are living beings born of and nurtured by a Living Earth. Real wealth is living wealth. Time is life. Money is just a number useful as a medium of exchange in well-regulated markets.

Life exists only in community. We humans are creatures of conscience who survive and prosper only as members of a Living Earth community. The prime task of any living community is to maintain the conditions essential to the life of its members. We all do best when we all do well in a world that works for all.

A connection to nature and community is essential to our physical and mental health and well-being. It is our nature to care and share for the benefit of all. Individualistic violence, greed, and ruthless competition are indicators of individual and social dysfunction. Environmental damage and extreme inequality are indicators of serious system failure.

The purpose of human institutions—whether business, government, or civil society—is to provide all people with the opportunity to make a healthy, meaningful living in a balanced co-productive relationship with Earth's community of life. Institutions designed to concentrate their decision-making power in the pursuit of purely financial ends unburdened by the exercise of human conscience—as is the case for most publicly traded limited-liability corporations—have no place in a healthy society.

Human institutions are human creations. That which humans create, humans can change.

Environmental sustainability, economic justice, and a living democracy are inseparable. We have all of them, or we have none of them.

As elaborated in the pages ahead, this story draws from the breadth of human knowledge, honors our interdependence with one another and with nature, recognizes the responsibilities that go with our human agency (the exercise of willful choice), gives our lives meaning, and guides our path to a just, sustainable, and democratic human future. It provides a framing vision for a Living Economy that:

- maintains a co-productive balance between humans and nature;

- provides a healthy, meaningful livelihood for all based on a just and equitable sharing of real wealth; and

- gives every person a voice in decisions on which their well-being and that of the whole depend.

I believe that the critical elements of this Sacred Life and Living Earth story live in the human heart. Largely unspoken, however, it has little public presence. To guide our path to a viable and prosperous human future, it must become our shared public story. This is our opportunity to make it so.

A MOMENT OF HOPE AND OPPORTUNITY

The institutional structures of corporate oligarchy have never seemed stronger. Yet in many ways, they have never been more vulnerable.[3] The foundation of their power is rapidly eroding as the seductive promises of the Sacred Money and Markets story lose their credibility and allure.

Although it is barely noticeable amid the daily news reports of spreading violence, environmental disaster, and political gridlock, and it is given no mention by corporate media, a new story is emerging in the words and deeds of millions of people engaged in rebuilding community and reconnecting with nature.

Voluntary simplicity, small houses, backyard and community gardens, and urban agriculture are all growing in popularity. The Living Building Challenge, which is driving the leading edge of the green building movement, shifts the building-industry frame from walling us off from one another and nature to increasing our connections with one another and nature. The New Economy movement, devoted to rebuilding local economies grounded in living-system principles and committed to creating an economy that works for all people and nature, is attracting rapidly expanding support—including support from local governments.

Scientists are acknowledging that animals are conscious and experience feeling states.[4] Campaigns against the factory farming of animals are gaining momentum. Local initiatives are removing pavement to restore turf and native plants.

Despite massive resistance from powerful corporate robots, environmental regulation is well established, and there is broad public support for government action to protect natural systems. Serious campaigns to strip corporations of their assumed rights of personhood and to establish in law the rights of nature are gaining strength.

The US Congress established the US Bureau of Reclamation in 1902 to build great dams to bend nature to our human will and use. The bureau's very name absurdly suggests its job is to reclaim from nature that which nature has taken from us. Now the US Bureau of Reclamation is removing dams to reclaim rivers for nature.

For a time in the decades following World War II, a privileged white middle class that felt well served by corporate rule provided corporations with a supportive political base. The institutions of the Money Economy that now systematically erode the white middle class erode as well their customer and political base and create an opening for social movements that unify the excluded.

For five thousand years, ruling classes have maintained their power by keeping the excluded divided along lines of race, gender, religion, language, ethnicity, and more. These lines are blurring. Universal education is increasing literacy and sophistication among the excluded. Communications technologies are facilitating links among grassroots movements. And intercultural exchange is building appreciation for the rich variety of our cultural traditions as a priceless asset.

Given the long history of racial and gender discrimination, the change in attitudes and laws relating to race and gender over the past sixty years is particularly dramatic. Despite strong undertones of prejudice in the venom of some politicians, an African American whom the law would have confined to the back of the bus in southern US states in the years of my youth became US president. Mainstream society now turns to indigenous people, once scorned as savages, as a source of wisdom and insight into how we all should live.

Demeaning racial and gender stereotypes widely accepted as immutable truth sixty years ago still exist, but their public expression now risks contempt and social sanction.

We are in the midst of a deep shift in human consciousness. The elements of its framing story are emerging. They have yet to find coherent, unifying expression.

CHANGE THE STORY, CHANGE THE FUTURE

We cannot act coherently as a society without a shared framing story. It defines our shared values and priorities, the questions we ask, and the options we consider. It shapes political debates, our institutions, and our interpretation of current events. For this reason, no matter how discredited an established story may be, we cling to it in our public discourse until it is replaced by a more compelling story.

Corporate interests repeat and reaffirm the Sacred Money and Markets story at every opportunity. They use it as the frame for every news report and political debate. They make it the basis of their legal arguments. They teach it in our schools and universities. So long as it carries the day, it defines our future.

Those of us committed to advancing justice, sustainability, peace, and democratic governance campaign and organize around individual issues—often defined by identity politics. In so doing, we concede the framing story and play into the divide-and-conquer strategy of elite politics.

Moreover, to the extent that we do argue our case within a larger story frame, it is most always the frame of the Sacred Money and Markets story. Thus, we do more than concede the story that legitimates the institutions responsible for the economic, social, environmental, and governance failures we seek to remedy. We reinforce it. We win occasional temporary victories for life on a particular issue, but we lose the future to money.

To win the future for life, we who would live in service to life must organize around the articulation and sharing of a compelling, unifying counterstory. We must make the articulation of a Sacred Life and Living Earth story a focal point of discussions in our living rooms, schools, churches, and civic centers. We must make our story the frame of our social media exchanges, community initiatives, and political advocacy. We must introduce it into academic curricula. We must use it in selecting the indicators by which we assess the performance of the economy.

We must discipline ourselves to recognize and challenge the fabricated Sacred Money and Markets story wherever we encounter it—in business news, in education, in political debates and advocacy, and in conversations with colleagues. Compel the champions of money to make their case within a Sacred Life and Living Earth frame.

In the pages ahead, we will explore the many dimensions

of the challenge of turning from a world organized around a Sacred Money and Markets story to a world organized around a Sacred Life and Living Earth story. We begin with the cosmologies that define our deepest beliefs about the nature of reality and our human origin, nature, and purpose.

2 OUR QUEST TO KNOW

Generally, the shared sacred story of a people aligns with their underlying cosmology or creation story—their deepest shared beliefs about the origin and nature of the universe. That we lack such a shared and currently credible foundational cosmology goes a long way toward explaining why we have been so easily seduced by the Sacred Money and Markets story.

A brief look at three familiar cosmologies—the Distant Patriarch, the Grand Machine, and the Mystical Unity—illustrates a range of answers to our deepest questions about where we come from and why. Each has its own implications for how we live. Each has its distinctive committed and vocal following. Each is in seeming conflict with the others. For a great many people none of them rings true. Corporate interests slip the fabricated Sacred Money and Markets story into the resulting void.

This chapter outlines critical elements of each of the familiar cosmologies and highlights their implications for how we think about agency, relationships, and meaning. It shows how the corporate PR machine draws from each of the familiar cosmologies to lend credibility to the Sacred Money and Markets story. Each in itself is incomplete, but they all contribute essential insights to the emerging Living Universe cosmology synthesis outlined in chapter 4.

Some readers will protest that my framing of one or more of the three cosmologies is too limiting and ignores their personally favored interpretation. True enough. Each has many variations, which would take volumes to explore fully. I seek here only to highlight the implications of the simplest, most influential, and most commonly recognized—some might say most caricatured—expression of each.

THE DISTANT PATRIARCH

As recited by the Abrahamic religions—Judaism, Christianity, and Islam—the Distant Patriarch cosmology begins with an all-knowing, all powerful god who, over a period of metaphorical days, created all that is—testing, assessing, and building on what he found good.

In the Distant Patriarch cosmology, God continues to rule his creation from his home in a separate, sacred dimension called heaven. From time to time, he lends a helping hand to the righteous, while observing and judging our obedience to his commandments handed down through sacred texts interpreted by religious authorities.

Since the beginning of empire, somewhere around 3000 BCE, variations of the Distant Patriarch cosmology have inspired billions of people, provided them with moral guidance, and focused attention on the prime importance of our individual relationship with a distant god of male gender.

For some believers, the distant patriarch is a loving god; for others he is jealous and vengeful. Either way the emphasis is on a personal relationship with a parent figure to whom believers appeal for help and salvation and whose rules set the boundaries of their lives. It holds a powerful attraction. It also tends to diminish the importance of our human relationships with, and dependence on, one another and nature.

Many believers in this cosmology maintain that God wants us to care for his creation; others see Earth only as a way station on the path to paradise. In this latter rendering, God grants humans dominion over nature during our brief Earthly layover.

For many fundamentalist believers, the Distant Patriarch cosmology reduces life to a fear-based quest to join the saved in heaven rather than the damned in hell. Life on Earth is a test of faith, a burden to be endured until our longed-for ascent to live with the creator in paradise. The resulting uncertainty and fear provide considerable scope for religious authorities to manipulate and exploit believers.

If an all-knowing and all-powerful god rules all that exists, then all that happens is by his will. Christian Calvinists concluded from this that the wealthy and powerful demonstrate thereby that they are God's chosen. To question their wealth and privilege is to question his judgment and will. The Sacred Money and Markets story picks up on this theme in its assertion that the rich merit special exemptions, tax breaks, and legal protections as the most productive and worthy among us.

THE GRAND MACHINE

The Grand Machine cosmology is associated with science. The contributions of science to human advancement and well-being, knowledge, and technology give this cosmology considerable authority and respect.

In the Grand Machine cosmology, the universe is much like a mechanical clock playing out its predetermined destiny as the tension in its spring winds down. By the reckoning of this cosmology, only the material is real. All physical phenomena are a consequence of some combination of physical mechanism and chance. Within this frame, life is merely an accidental outcome of material complexity and has no larger meaning or purpose. Consciousness is an artifact of physical processes in the brain. Free will and agency are illusions.

This limited and badly outdated lens has had serious cultural consequences. Most particularly, it has long limited the biological sciences to explaining life's extraordinary capacity for cooperative, intelligent self-direction as solely the consequence of an individualistic competition for survival, territory, and reproductive advantage. Sometimes referred to as social Darwinism, this frame has provided a pseudo-scientific justification for colonial imperialism, racial domination, rapacious capitalism, and market fundamentalism.

Economists embraced this outdated social Darwinist

frame to support the simplistic assumption that we humans are by nature individualistic competitors and that unrestrained competition drives human progress and prosperity to maximize the well-being of all. Particularly pernicious is the idea that human will (agency) is an illusion.

The underlying intellectual frame of the Grand Machine cosmology strips our existence of meaning and purpose and undermines our sense of moral responsibility for one another and nature. The related and still widely embraced social Darwinist frame suggests that we either dominate nature and other humans or become victims of their domination over us. We are left in a state of existential despair searching for sources of distraction from the terrifying loneliness of a meaningless existence in a hostile universe.

Propagandists in the employ of corporate interests step in with their Sacred Money and Markets story to assure us that shopping and competition for money, financial status, and material status symbols can fill our need for meaning, purpose, and relationships. These pursuits become addictive distractions. They do not—and cannot—provide true fulfillment no matter how obsessively we pursue them.

Organizationally the social Darwinist lens denies the possibility of democratic communities that self-organize around caring relationships. This leaves only two options: centralized public authority or the market. Both are subject to control by money-seeking corporate robots relieved of responsibility for their morally corrupt behavior by an economic ideology posing as a science.

We do not lack for examples of the human capacity for

greed and ruthless competition in disregard for the well-being of others. Such behavior, however, is a mark of psychopathic and sociopathic dysfunction. Emotionally healthy humans are characteristically caring and sharing—traits essential to healthy social function.

Although the Grand Machine and Distant Patriarch cosmologies present sharply contrasting perspectives, they both support, in subtle and not so subtle ways, three self-destructive characteristics of contemporary society: First, a concentration of institutional power in global corporations and financial markets. Second, a divisive individualism that creates the illusion of freedom in the midst of corporate tyranny. Third, a utilitarian view of life that drives moral decline and strips our existence of meaning.

The most compelling challenge to the mechanistic lens of the Grand Machine cosmology comes from within science itself. The findings of quantum physics describe a decidedly nonmechanist reality in which seemingly solid objects are mostly empty space sparsely populated by oddly entangled particles—some of which, depending on the observer, may act like waves. By this reckoning, what we experience as solid matter is largely an illusion generated by self-organizing relationships among particles difficult to explain solely in terms of mechanism and chance.

Such findings are so at odds with our perceptual experience as to have real meaning only to the most advanced scientists and mathematicians. For most of us, they have no implications—moral or otherwise. We therefore enclose them in a separate mental space reserved for curious but largely irrelevant facts.

THE MYSTICAL UNITY

The Mystical Unity cosmology has ancient roots in the world's spiritual traditions. It is most commonly and explicitly associated with Buddhism. In the classic expression of this cosmology, what we experience as material reality—including our experience of ourselves as material beings—is an illusion generated by the human ego that separates us from the reality of the eternal oneness from which we manifest.

Buddhists use the relationship between the ocean and the wave as a metaphor for our personal relationship to the eternal. The wave has its own temporary identity, seemingly distinct from the ocean from which it manifests. It exists, however, only as an expression of the ocean.

Teachers in the Mystical Unity tradition generally focus on a first-person experience of awakening through meditation to the infinite love and peace that lie beyond the perceived and often violent world of our daily experience.

The Mystical Unity cosmology is consonant with the deepest human spiritual experience and fulfills our deep need for belonging. Quantum physics in large measure affirms its assertion that all being is interconnected and that matter is an illusion. There are profound insights in the tradition's recognition that all beings are inextricably connected and co-emergent; that the harm we do to others, we do as well to ourselves; and that the veil of illusion is a source of suffering and violence.

Typically, practitioners of Mystical Unity teach that the path to ending violence is to suppress and transcend the ego through meditative practice and thereby to experience and meld our individualized awareness with the eternal oneness. For some followers, the commitment to radical nonviolence leads to non-engagement. They do not hold dominator institutions accountable for the violence inflicted against life. Instead, they say that those who attempt to hold them accountable are "othering" the persons who serve those institutions. Othering, they explain, is an expression of the ego, a denial of the oneness of being, a denial of the essential goodness of those persons, and therefore a disruptive act of violence.

This illuminates a paradox. The quest of an individual to deny or escape the ego in search of personal peace and tranquility while studiously denying personal responsibility for addressing the institutions that inflict unconscionable suffering on others is itself an act of ego.

Change is afoot. As described by Kurt Johnson and David Ord in *The Coming Interspiritual Age*, there is a growing sentiment among followers of the Mystical Unity tradition that the call is not to "wake up and detach." Rather it is to "wake up and engage" in order to create a global civilization that recognizes the unity of our being and common purpose.[1] The international Buddhist leader and activist Sulak Sivaraksa advocates an explicit recognition within Buddhist spiritual and social teaching of the ways in which major institutions, most notably transnational corporations, encourage and reward violence against life.[2]

From the perspective of the challenges of daily life, discussions and debates about cosmology can seem abstract and pointless. Only rarely do we notice the powerful political implications of our deepest beliefs—even of our denial of belief.

Contesting cosmologies have gone hand in hand with contesting power structures throughout human history. A brief overview of the history of story politics will highlight the central significance of our current story politics.

3 A BRIEF HISTORY OF STORY POLITICS

We humans have a deep need for meaning, for answers to the ultimate questions. In their pursuit of answers, prophets, sages, and wisdom keepers of all times and traditions have recognized a spiritual order and unity in creation that defies description. Necessarily, they communicate their insights through simple stories and familiar images within the context of their time and place. Such stories shape both individual and collective behavior.

Different stories prevail in wondrous variety at different times in different places in a continuously evolving process. As stories and images pass from generation to generation and travel from place to place, critical nuances may be lost or modified. Followers may forget that the original stories and images were metaphorical, not literal. Power holders favor and promote interpretations that serve their interests.

This chapter presents a big-picture overview of the politics of our human search for meaning. It puts into context the work at hand of replacing a fabricated Sacred Money and Markets story that legitimates rule by money-seeking corporate robots with an authentic Sacred Life and Living

Earth story that reawakens us to our true nature as living beings born of a Living Earth and creates a context for a radical living democracy.

INDIGENOUS PEOPLES

The earliest peoples were hunter-gatherers who lived by harvesting the gifts of nature. Their lives were inseparable from the life of nature. They honored Earth as their living mother, a community of life, and the source of their birth and nurture. They studied the ways of their sacred Earth Mother and her many children with reverence and respect. Their most revered members were those who possessed special abilities to mediate the tribe's relationship with the spirits that animated all being. In the cosmology common to most indigenous peoples, all being is conscious, intelligent, and alive.

RELIGION

With time, humans took up settled cultivation and formed larger and more stratified social units. The metaphors by which these early agricultural societies understood the animating spirit of creation evolved accordingly. The people of these societies continued to depend on nature, but their lives gradually disconnected from hers.

As kings and emperors established their rule, the metaphors changed. People of this time assumed that, just as the human world had its powerful rulers, so too did the spirit world. Earthly rulers commonly believed themselves to be representatives, even incarnations, of spirit-world deities.

Gender-balanced societies worshiped both a Sky Father and an Earth Mother. Matrilineal societies favored feminine metaphors and worshiped feminine deities. Patriarchal societies favored masculine metaphors and worshiped masculine deities.

The Abrahamic faiths—Judaism, Christianity, Islam—emerged within male-dominated societies. They quite naturally favored the Sky Father and dismissed goddess worship as primitive and pagan. Their priestly classes secured their authority by declaring certain ancient texts to be the word of God and subject to their exclusive interpretation. The world divided into diverse institutionalized religious sects and subsects prone to engage in a deadly competition for followers (and power) based on the premise that "my god is the only true god." For much of the history of what we think of as Western civilization, the word of the church was canon law, with often dire consequences for those who disobeyed.

THE MYSTICS

Each of the Abrahamic faiths had its mystics who discerned creation as the material manifestation of an undifferentiated spiritual unity rather than the handiwork of an aging patriarch who lives apart from his creation. The cosmologies of Western mystics bore more than a passing resemblance to those of the mystics of Eastern religious traditions, particularly of Buddhism and Hinduism, who make little distinction between humans and nature. In Western societies that emphasize the separation of humans from nature, mystics enjoyed pockets of popular support but little institutional sponsorship. If God is an inner spirit, then there is no need for a priesthood to intermediate.

SCIENCE

The modern conflict between science and religion is most evident in the United States, where a constitutional separation of church and state has resulted in the legally mandated exclusion of religious teachings from public school curricula. This creates a backlash from those who look to scripture as their defining authority and believe that the science view of evolution and the age of the universe conflicts with scriptural teaching.

We easily forget that the major figures to whom we look as the founders of Western science—including Copernicus, Galileo, Kepler, and Newton—did not set out to challenge or undermine religion. Most considered themselves devout Christians, although Galileo explicitly challenged the authority of the Catholic Church and Newton held unorthodox views on the trinity and other matters theological.

In 1543, the Renaissance astronomer Nicolaus Copernicus published his thesis asserting that, contrary to church teaching and the prevailing belief of his time, the sun and planets do not circle Earth. Rather, Earth is one of several planets that circle the sun. For nearly six decades, the Copernican thesis aroused little interest or controversy—until Galileo became its champion and the Catholic Church recognized it as a threat to its foundational doctrine that Earth is the orbital center of all celestial bodies and humans are the center of God's attention.

The subsequent attack from the Church pressed scientists to clearly differentiate themselves from religious dogma and secure their own authority by rigorous adherence to a narrowly defined scientific method characterized by disciplined observation, quantification, mathematical models, and an insistence that material mechanism and chance hold the only acceptable explanation for observed phenomena.

This discipline brought rigor to the search for order in the universe and lifted human understanding and technological possibility to previously unimagined levels. The focus on material mechanism, however, led to a denial of agency— the presence of conscious, intelligent choice making. It also supported the division of knowledge into narrowly defined fields of specialization at the expense of our ability to study and understand the workings of complex systems.

Much as the priestly classes of institutionalized Western religions generally forgot that the patriarch was a metaphor, the institutional gatekeepers of science sometimes forget that denial of the existence of agency is a methodological choice, not a finding. To this day, despite extraordinary advances in the physical, biological, and brain sciences, most scientists feel compelled to explain observed data within a mechanistic reductionist frame that denies or ignores conscious intelligence. Such a dangerously partial view of reality conflicts with our need for a fuller understanding of our nature as living beings—and with the actual beliefs of many scientists.[1]

SIX BLIND MEN AND AN ELEPHANT

Our current situation brings to mind the parable of six blind men attempting to discern the nature of an elephant.[2] The first feels its side and proclaims, "An elephant is like a wall." The second touches its tusk and counters, "No, it is like a spear." The third feels the trunk and says, "Truly it is like a snake." The fourth rubs a leg and insists, "An elephant is like a tree." The fifth feels its ear and pronounces it to be "like a fan." The sixth grasps the tail and says, "Nonsense, an elephant is like a rope."

Each of the blind men discerns a piece of a larger truth easily misinterpreted when taken out of its context. Only by sharing and synthesizing their individual insights do the blind men have any prospect of accurately describing the external qualities of the elephant. It is particularly telling that by focusing on the elephant's physical characteristics, their descriptions give no hint of the internal essence of the elephant as an intelligent living being of complex emotions and many talents.

We might think of this parable as a metaphor for scientists examining the universe. The tools of modern science give scientists an unprecedented ability to view it in intimate detail. But the greater the focus on detail, the easier it is to miss the nature and essence of the whole.

The Distant Patriarch and Mystical Unity cosmologies each contribute an understanding of the deeper essence ignored by the Grand Machine cosmology. Yet, without the contribution of science, they fail to capture the true wonder of the universe.

Throughout most of the human experience, individuals grew up taking for granted the shared cosmology of the culture into which they were born. Contemporary society presents us with a cacophony of seemingly competing choices. It is a moment of confusion and conflict in which our sense of ethical mooring has slipped away.

Purveyors of the Sacred Money and Markets story have stepped into the void, making selective reference to one or another of the readily recognized cosmologies as suits their purpose. "God wants you to be rich." "Competition for survival drives evolutionary progress." "Consumption is the path to happiness." Corporate-sponsored media and most academic economists constantly reinforce the underlying story frame.

Perhaps the most dangerous premise of the Sacred Money and Markets story is the conceit that with enough money our human technologies will liberate us from a dependence on nature. Therefore we need not see to her care. For a time the frontiers of science and technology appeared to confirm this conceit, particularly as scientists assured us that they were only one missing energy particle away from a complete understanding of everything—another human conceit since shattered as science confronts the extent to which the deepest mysteries continue to elude us.

CONFRONTING THE UNKNOWN

The current frontier of science is the expanding recognition of the staggering limitations of our human understanding of how and why the universe evolves toward ever-increasing complexity, beauty, awareness, and possibility.

Science now concludes that the universe contains hundreds of billions of galaxies, each with hundreds of billions of stars. Yet in total, their observed matter accounts for only 4 percent of what scientists calculate to be the total mass of the universe. Beyond vague and untested theories about dark energy and dark matter, scientists have no idea what constitutes the other 96 percent.[3]

Until recently, science assumed that DNA provided a mechanistic explanation for the growth of living organisms from inception to maturity—and that it dictated much, if not all, of their behavior. It also assumed that 98 percent of human DNA was "junk," because scientists could not associate it with specific essential functions.

Recent studies suggest that much of the "junk" DNA may actually have essential functions and that these functions may be goal oriented and involve active learning. Some scientists further suggest that genetic codes cannot alone explain the intricate variations in the physical design and function of living organisms.

Biologists have traditionally focused on the classification and study of individual species, giving limited attention to the dynamic organization and unfolding resilience and adaptation of the larger communities within which these species have evolved. This too is changing. A growing frontier of biology is the in-depth study of life's organization into complex, self-organizing living communities. Among the most fascinating of these communities are those populated by invisible microbial life essential to human health and well-being.

We know there are more microorganisms (bacteria, fungi, algae, protozoa, and nematodes) in a teaspoon of healthy living soil than there are people on Earth. Each individual and species is engaged in an active, interdependent, self-directing exchange essential to the health and fertility of the soils that grow our food. Similarly, vast numbers of nonhuman microorganisms inhabit our human skin, genital area, mouth, and intestines and work in co-productive partnership with our human cells, which depend on the microorganisms for essential functions.[4]

Biologists have only begun to identify and catalog the vast variety of these microorganisms, let alone understand their varied functions and the methods of their self-organization, adaptation, and co-evolution. Yet we do not hesitate in our attempt to control these natural dynamics through genetic modification, antibiotics, antiseptics, and pesticides with only the most limited understanding of the ultimate consequences.

We had best not presume we can control, dominate, or free ourselves from dependence on that which we are only beginning to understand. Indeed, the more we learn about what we don't know, the greater our recognition of the extraordinary complexity and intelligence of the processes that birthed us. The greater this recognition, the stronger is the case for tempering our sense of exceptionalism with appropriate humility.

A MOMENT OF OPPORTUNITY

These are frightening times. We see a future in which the evolutionary viability of our species is in doubt. Our most powerful and respected institutions are driving rather than resolving the unfolding crisis. Our familiar but narrowly defined and seemingly competing cosmologies lack contemporary credibility.

The Sacred Money and Markets story has prevailed as our familiar but narrowly defined and competing cosmologies lost credibility. That story is in turn losing its credibility as awareness spreads that its premises are immoral, illogical, and at odds with both science and our daily experience.

The work of our time is to learn to live in alignment with the structures and processes of a Living Earth. We must reinvent our future. This requires that we reinvent our sacred story and the institutions that structure our relationships of power.

The less credible our established story and institutions, the greater the opportunity to replace them with a story and institutions better aligned with our needs and understanding. Ours is a moment of opportunity unprecedented in the human experience to reinvent our story, our institutions, and our future with conscious collective intention.

Living Earth is not simply a poetic turn of phrase. It is a pragmatic, evidence-based statement of truth with profound implications.

A discernible outline of a new Living Universe cosmology is emerging from the chaos and despair. It melds insights from the Distant Patriarch, Grand Machine, Mystical Unity, and indigenous Living Earth cosmologies to more adequately capture the grandeur, complexity, and mystery of creation than any of those more familiar cosmologies reveals by itself.[5]

The Living Universe cosmology describes a universe that bears far more resemblance to a seed bursting forth to express itself as a magnificent flowering tree than to a mechanical clock running down as its spring unwinds. It provides the foundational frame for a Sacred Life and Living Earth story that in turn frames a Living Economy for a Living Earth.

4   A LIVING UNIVERSE

Within little more than the life span of my generation, an
explosive growth in human population and consumption
has combined with breathtaking advances in human
knowledge and technology to change the world almost beyond recognition. We look inward to observe the behavior
of subatomic particles and the inner processes of individual
living cells. We peer far into space to discern the workings of
the universe and the dynamic processes of its unfolding. We
look back on our own big history to describe in ever more
magnificent detail the dynamic processes underlying the
evolution of life on Earth.

With this extraordinary perspective, we can see Earth
as a wondrous, resilient, adaptive living being to which we
must adapt—or die.[1]

The most advanced observations of physical systems by
quantum physics and of biological systems by the life sciences reveal extraordinary capacities for self-organization,
even in seemingly solid matter. Mechanism and chance are
clearly involved. It is increasingly evident that there is also
a third element—intelligent self-organization—of which we

**DIFFERENT COSMOLOGIES,
DIFFERENT WORLDVIEWS**

Each of the four contrasting cosmologies convey a very different understanding of relationships, agency, and meaning.

1. **Distant Patriarch**: My most important relationship is to a distant God who is the source of all agency and meaning.

2. **Grand Machine**: I exist in a mechanistically interconnected cosmos devoid of agency and possessing no purpose or meaning.

3. **Mystical Unity**: Relationships, agency, and meaning are all artifacts of the illusion of separation created by ego; I am one with the timeless eternal One.

4. **Living Universe**: I am an intelligent, self-directing participant in a conscious, interconnected self-organizing cosmos on a journey of self-discovery toward ever greater complexity, beauty, awareness, and possibility.

have only the most elemental understanding. It may be the most important.

The more we learn, the more it seems the metaphor of organism is far more apt than the metaphor of mechanism as the lens through which to view the epic unfolding of the universe.

We now have the elements of a new cosmology with ancient roots that provides a firm foundation for a Sacred Life and Earth Community story. It in turn frames our search for a Living Economy that works in co-productive partnership with Earth's community of life.

EPIC JOURNEY

According to science, the universe was born some 13.8 billion years ago when a giant energy cloud burst forth in a blinding flash. By fortunate coincidence, it had exactly the right physical constants to form into quantum particles that formed into complex atoms that formed into complex molecules.[2]

With the passing of time, these molecules formed into trillions of burning stars, each comprising an unimaginably vast number of quantum particles, atoms, and molecules in constant, often violent, and chaotic interaction. These stars produced and threw off substances we experience as stable solid matter, yet which quantum science tells us is mostly empty space occupied by constantly moving, appearing, and disappearing waves and particles.

Many of the trillions of stars birthed and provided a sustained energy source for the planets that circled them. At least one of these trillions of planets possessed exactly the right conditions for the emergence of simple organisms with the ability to co-evolve into ever more complex organisms.

These organisms happened to interact with the planet's geological forces to transform and stabilize the chemical composition of the planet's atmosphere, lower the planet's temperature, concentrate and sequester a vast variety of chemical compounds, and create weather systems that provided the planet's land mass with continuously renewing supplies of freshwater and oxygen-rich air. This self-regulating system now maintains the chemical composition of sea and air, air pressure, and surface temperatures and climate stability consistent with the needs of Earth's widely varied species. These conditions contrast starkly with those of Earth's planetary neighbors and represent a state that scientists call thermodynamic disequilibrium, or negative entropy (active flows of matter and energy).[3]

DEEP INTENTION

The idea that this miracle is solely the outcome of a combination of mechanics and purposeless chance defies logic, common sense, and the foundational principles of Newtonian mechanics.

Scientific observation, indigenous wisdom, and the revelations of religious and contemplative practice each add to our understanding of the wonder and genius of creation. Put it all together and we begin to discern a Living Universe cosmology that evokes a radical vision of deep intentionality and purpose. For humans it evokes a possibility of radical democracy.

Individual interpretations of the data will vary. As the elements of the emerging cosmology come together for me, what humans experience as a physical universe is the product of a spiritual consciousness seeking to know itself by manifesting in an unfolding creative journey of self-discovery. The spirit, possessed of an insatiable drive, burst forth as the vast energy cloud described by astrophysicists. The same drive to become, and to know and express our possibilities, is a defining quality of our species.

In *The Science of Oneness* Malcolm Hollick draws from teachings of the Gnostics, who believed that consciousness, not matter, is the fundamental essence of reality. "Without the conscious experience of living, we would be unaware of existence; nothing would exist for us, and we would not exist for ourselves. . . . I, the subject, am only conscious when there is something, an object, of which I am aware. . . . Consciousness only came into being when the primal Mystery divided into two—Consciousness and its object. . . . The unknowable became aware of itself as both knower and known, observer and observed, witness and experience."[4] The material manifestation is in a sense an illusion, but a purposeful one.

By the reckoning of the Living Universe cosmology, all things—all beings—including stars, planets, humans, animals, plants, rocks, and rivers—are both expression and agent of the spirit, each with its place and purpose in an epic journey. Earth and the material universe of human experience are more than the spirit's creation; they are its manifestation. The spirit is in the world, and the world is in the spirit.

Religious scholars would say the spirit is both immanent and transcendent, a concept they call panentheism. In his expression of his Jewish faith, Jesus taught, "The kingdom is within." Muhammad taught, "Wherever you turn, there is the face of Allah."

Within this frame, the ego and the illusion of separation by which we experience our individual identity are essential to our ability to contribute to the quest of the spirit to know itself.

Among all the species known to us, we humans are clearly distinctive in our capacity for agency and thereby our ability to shape with conscious intention both our own future and that of Earth's community of life. Used with a sense of creative responsibility, our distinctive human talents can be a blessing for all. Used as a license for individual excess, they become a deadly threat to all, as we now so dramatically demonstrate. The cause of this misdirection is not an inherent flaw in our nature; it is a flaw in our story.

DISTRIBUTED AGENCY

Agency is the power to choose. In the classic Distant Patriarch cosmology, agency is exclusive to a god external to the universe. In the classic Grand Machine and Mystical Unity cosmologies, agency is an illusion. In the Living Universe cosmology, agency is intrinsic, distributed, and pervasive and essential to the creative learning that expresses itself as the universe unfolds.

It is a well-established finding in the field of group dynamics that team decision making is more creative and effective in dealing with complex problems than an individual decision maker. The theory of distributed intelligence suggests that multiple interlinked minds have capabilities inherently greater than a single mind. For a great many tasks, an interlinked cluster of personal computers can be more efficient and more powerful than a single supercomputer.

This same creative potential of interconnected agents acting as interconnecting self-directing systems expresses itself throughout the universe. Living Earth is an extraordinary example. So too is the individual human body.

Like you, I am but one of the many trillions of organisms that make up the biosphere, Earth's exquisitely complex, resilient, and continuously evolving community of life.

My body, like yours, is a complex living community; it is my most intimate example of the potential of a distributed intelligence for creative self-organization. It comprises tens of trillions of individual choice-making cells, each engaged in managing its own health and integrity under changing and often stressful circumstances. In addition to the tens of trillions of cells that form its vital organs and physical structure, the body hosts an even greater number of nonhuman microorganisms that provide an endless variety of services essential to its health in return for their own sustenance.

Each cell functions as a member of a self-regulating community that maintains to the best of its ability the health and integrity of the living being that expresses itself as our conscious, thinking, choice-making body. Even under conditions of extreme stress and deprivation, these cells self-organize to fight off a vast variety of invasive viruses, cancer cells, and pathogenic bacteria that pose threats to the health of the whole.

They adapt to changing temperatures and to variations in the body's intake of food and water. They heal damaged tissues and collect and provide essential sensory data to the body's conscious mind. They mobilize instantly to respond to external threats, in some instances even before the conscious mind recognizes them.

All the while, these trillions of cells continuously replace themselves, with no loss of the integrity of the body and its function. The cells lining the human stomach replace themselves every 5 days. The surface of the skin regenerates every 14 days. Red blood cells renew approximately every 120 days.[5]

The result is a constantly regenerating physical being with a capacity for extraordinary feats of physical grace and intellectual acuity far beyond the capability—and presumably the imagination—of any individual cell or microorganism.

The wonder and implications of this process are breathtaking. Visualize your body continuously re-creating itself in a constant exchange of energy, nutrients, water, and information with Earth, in which Earth's microorganisms serve as intermediaries. It is the ultimate intimacy. Like a flowing river, my body maintains its distinctive individual form, abilities, and memories without loss or disruption even though its matter and energy are in constant flow and exchange within and beyond itself.

Furthermore, these miraculous self-directing processes mostly occur far below the level of my conscious awareness. So long as I provide the essentials of nutrition, hydration, rest, and exercise, my cells fulfill their responsibilities to maintain my body's healthy function without specific instructions from any central decision-making authority that we know of.

Cells can and do go rogue and become a threat to the whole. Cancer is an example. The healthy cells self-organize to eliminate them. If they fail, the body dies and the rogue cells thus self-eliminate.

We might take this as a warning. We humans are behaving as rogue cells in the body of Living Earth and have activated Earth's defenses, notably climate change and deadly infectious diseases.

To achieve our individual and species potential and secure our common future, we must align with the wisdom and intention of the spirit that manifests through us. In the most mature expression of our human consciousness, we develop a capacity to recognize and honor simultaneously both our oneness and our individuality. It helps us achieve spiritual understanding, accept responsibility for the consequences of our personal choices, and create an economy that meets the needs of all members of Earth's self-sustaining community of life.

LEVELS OF CONSCIOUSNESS

So what is the relationship between our individual human consciousness and the meta-consciousness of the whole? The relationship between the individual cells of my body and my conscious mind suggests an answer.

Through the findings of science, I know my body's cells exist. I consciously care about their health, because I know that my own health depends on their health. Even if I had the capacity to consciously discern and care for a single cell, however, I could not possibly track and care for each of the tens of trillions of cells that make up my body. Think of the distraction.

My body's capacity for intelligent choice resides at the cellular level far below my conscious awareness for good reason. My body's meta-consciousness—as distinct from the consciousness of an individual cell or organ—is free to concentrate on managing my body's relationship to the world beyond the boundary of my skin, decisions beyond the ability of any individual cell.

My body's meta-consciousness thus establishes the context of the self-managed choice making of the individual cells. The cells take it from there, allowing my conscious mind the freedom to engage in creative inquiry and expression.

Scale this logic up to the cosmic level. If we assume a Living Universe meta-consciousness, it is unlikely it could attend individually to each of the trillions of celestial entities that constitute it—just as I cannot attend to each of the cells of my body.

This is not to suggest that the meta-consciousness is indifferent to our human existence. The meta-consciousness may care for us with the love that some believe to be the binding force of the universe. In the deepest sense, it likely does possess an awareness and concern for our individual well-being—but not in the way suggested by the traditional Distant Patriarch cosmology.

If each human is a choice-making manifestation of the spirit, we are each an instrument of the spirit's awareness and agency.

This suggests that the voice that may reply to my conscious mind in the course of meditation or prayer is both my voice *and* the voice of the meta-consciousness that expresses itself through me. My appeal to God for guidance or for relief from my suffering is thus in effect an appeal to myself to act with wisdom and self-awareness while remaining mindful of my responsibility to and for the larger evolving community to which I belong.

Similarly, as I step back to view with awe and wonder the creative magnificence of the universe unfolding, perhaps I serve as an instrument by which the meta-consciousness steps back to view and reflect on itself.

A DREAM IN THE HUMAN HEART

In private conversations, I find the Living Universe cosmology is largely consistent with the private—if rarely spoken—cosmology of many scientists, practicing members of varied faiths, and people who define themselves as spiritual but not necessarily religious. I have come to suspect that some version of this story lives in every human heart—no matter how suppressed it may be.

Traditional indigenous wisdom keepers speak of the creator's Original Instructions to humans to get along with one another and nature.[6] Science now affirms that the human brain evolved to reward cooperation, service, and compassion. Our brains are wired to connect.[7] Developmental psychologists who study the maturing of the human consciousness find that at our most mature, it is our nature to feel a deep connection with and caring for all being.

Systems biologists find that the healthy function of any living system depends on collaboration. Most all living organisms exist, thrive, and co-evolve only within living communities engaged in a continuous synergistic sharing and exchange that from a big-picture perspective is fundamentally cooperative.[8]

The Original Instructions are integral to our human nature, and they manifest through the whole of life. This comes as no surprise to anyone who is paying attention. It is evident from our daily experience that caring relationships are an essential foundation of the healthy human families and communities that are in turn essential to our individual health and happiness.

Extreme individualism, greed, and violence are pathological; their expression indicates physical, developmental, cultural, and/or institutional system failure.

We are creatures born of an evolving Living Universe on a quest. To guide us to our place of contribution to that quest, it seems we are born with a dream in our heart of a world beyond individualism, greed, and violence.

It is a dream to which countless generations have aspired. It is a dream long deferred by our missteps as we explored all the possibilities of our nature for both good (that which serves life) and evil (that which destroys life).

It is a dream of peace and creative prosperity for all. It is the dream of living democracies, self-governing communities in which we together envision and shape our common future. It is the vision of self-organizing local markets in which we provision ourselves through fair and equal exchange. It is a dream that aligns with the evolutionary trajectory of a Living Universe toward ever-greater complexity, beauty, awareness, and possibility.

It was the dream of a young Jewish teacher named Jesus who long ago threw the moneychangers from the temple of life. It was the dream of Martin Luther King Jr. and the freedom riders of the civil rights movement, of Gandhi, and of Nelson Mandela.

Science is now confirming what we feel in our heart and daily experience. People who organize their lives around money and consumption to the exclusion of living relationships are prone to depression, anxiety, and low self-esteem compensated for by obscene displays of extravagance.

We experience the fullness of life through the caring relationships of close friends and healthy caring families and communities and the positive rush we experience when helping a neighbor, volunteering, and giving. A connection with nature is essential to our health and happiness. We thrive in jobs that allow us to express creativity, exercise initiative, and be of service to others.

In their book, *The Spirit Level*, the British epidemiologists Richard Wilkinson and Kate Pickett provide an exhaustive review of research on the relationship between wealth equality and indicators of physical, mental, and social health and happiness. On virtually every indicator, societies that are more equitable enjoy more positive outcomes than those that are less equitable. The healthiest societies are not those that have more income, more money—or even more education. They are those that are most giving and loving, societies that share what they have most equitably.[9]

From a Living Earth perspective, our human birth was no accident. It involved a great deal of preparation. That we are born of Earth with a dream in our heart of caring and sharing to the benefit of all strongly suggests that the Living Universe did not birth Earth to serve us. Rather Living Earth birthed us to serve its continued evolutionary unfolding.

5 CHILDREN OF
A LIVING EARTH

To paraphrase and expand on Carl Sagan: If you wish to make a human from scratch, you must first invent a Living Universe that in turn births a Living Earth. An ambitious undertaking, it took 13.8 billion years.

The Living Universe had to get a great many conditions right to create a home for humans. None of the three familiar cosmologies captures the true wonder of this miracle or the significance of our need to honor and maintain the conditions essential to our own existence.

The fabricated Sacred Money and Markets story misses, even denies, our dependence on Living Earth. The authentic Sacred Life and Living Earth story embraces this dependence and the implications for how we humans organize to make our living.

THE 3.8-BILLION-YEAR MIRACLE OF ORGANIC LIFE

Scientists estimate that there may be as many as 40 billion habitable Earth-size planets in the galaxy.[1] Carbon-based life has likely emerged on others. We are only certain, however, that it has emerged on one. We still have only the vaguest idea of how it happened.

To our best understanding, the evolution of carbon-based Earth life has been a long and difficult journey of more than 3.8 billion years. The first 2 billion belonged to a tightly networked community of prokaryotes, single-cell organisms with no nucleus (bacteria are one type). Through their interactions, they invented all of life's essential miniaturized chemical systems and transformed Earth's surface and atmosphere to create the conditions that subsequently supported increasingly complex organisms.[2] Undeterred by catastrophic mass extinctions, Earth's evolving community of life regularly recovered and restored its trajectory toward ever increasing complexity, beauty, awareness, and possibility.

Throughout the journey, Earth's countless and ever more varied organisms captured and shared energy, water, and nutrients in interaction with Earth's physical systems to create and then to continuously regenerate Earth's soils, rivers, aquifers, fisheries, forests, grasslands, and much more. Most every living organism, no matter how small and seemingly unimportant, earns its living contributing to the health, resilience, and creative potential of the whole. All the while, they together maintain a climatic balance and atmosphere suited to the needs of the community's individual members.

Acting as a community in concert with Earth's physical structures and forces, Earth's diverse species filtered excess carbon and a vast variety of toxins from Earth's air, waters, and soils and sequestered them deep underground. In so doing—whether by luck or deep cosmic intention—they created environmental conditions necessary for the birth of a species with a capacity for conscious, creative, self-reflective choice far beyond any other.

In a collective trance induced by the idolatrous Sacred Money and Markets story, we of that species now devote our best minds and technologies to extracting and releasing those sequestered carbons and toxins back into Earth's atmosphere, waters, and soils as money-seeking corporate robots exploit and suppress Earth's natural processes to make a quick buck. Our acceptance of this insanity is the ultimate demonstration of the potentially fatal consequence of living by a fabricated Sacred Money and Markets story.

BIRTH, REBELLION, AND THE STEP TO SPECIES MATURITY

Earth birthed our species some two hundred thousand years ago. We acknowledged our dependence on her and honored her as our sacred Earth Mother. Our sense of separation began around 3000 BCE with the rise of imperial civilizations. It accelerated over the most recent four hundred years as modern science began to advance our godlike powers to manipulate, suppress, and exploit her. In our forgetfulness of what we are and whence we came, we behave as our Earth Mother's prodigal children acting out in adolescent rebellion.

As is common for adolescents, our ability to reshape our world developed faster than our capacity to act with wisdom and emotional maturity. With a naive sense of invincibility, we recklessly tested the limits of our newfound abilities, unmindful that special abilities come with special responsibilities.

Hope lies in the evidence that we are reawakening to what I believe to be a fundamental truth of our existence. We humans, like all other beings, are both product and instrument of creation, not its purpose. We belong to Earth, and our health and well-being are inseparable from her health and well-being.

IT TAKES A LIVING COMMUNITY

The wonder of organic (carbon-based) life is that each and every living organism, from the individual cell to Living Earth, maintains itself in an internal state of active, adaptive, resilient, creative thermodynamic disequilibrium in seeming violation of the basic principle of entropy—the loss of ordered structure. It takes a community of organic life to maintain the conditions required by carbon-based life. Maintaining the conditions of its own existence is the prime task of every living community and each of its members.

Science has only the sketchiest idea of how it works beyond a recognition that organic life depends on a continuous flow of energy, water, nutrients, and information. To maintain these flows, life self-organizes everywhere as a system of bioregional communities that scale upward like nested Russian dolls from the micro to the global. Some systems theorists refer to this as a holonic structure—a system of nested whole parts.

It is a critical though seldom noted insight that individual cells and organisms can no more exist outside a larger community of living organisms than the community of life can exist without the self-directing agency of the individuals that constitute it. The more complex, diverse, and coherent are the relationships internal to each community, the greater the community's resilience and creative potential.

As individual organisms and species evolve in community, they learn to meet their own needs in ways that ultimately contribute to the generative capacities of the whole. As each individual and species has a responsibility to contribute, so too does each have the right to share in the community's product.

Although the competitive aspect of life's evolution has dominated Western attention since the studies of Darwin, shared spaces create shared destinies and interests that reward the formation of synergistic relationships among individuals and species.[3] In the frame of the life-centered "new biology," the species that succeed and thrive over the long term are those that find their place of service to the whole. Whether this is a conscious process for any other species, we may never know. For humans, given the combination of our dominance and our extraordinary capacity for agency, it is essential that the process be conscious and intentional.

FROM ABUSER TO HEALER

A growing body of evidence suggests that humans are now the dominant force shaping the generative systems that sustain Earth as a living being. Thus, some refer to our geologic time as the Anthropocene—the epoch of the human.

Environmentalists point to our need to learn to live within the limits of Earth's capacity to sustain our consumption. Discussion of these limits, however, is generally within a mechanistic frame, as if we were dealing with a machine with an unvarying capacity to pump water, produce food, or stabilize the climate.

Earth, however, is not a machine. She is a living organism. Her abundance and ability to support human life depends on the health of her complex and interdependent living systems. The more we abuse her, the poorer her health, and the less abundant her soils, rivers, aquifers, forests, fisheries, and grasslands. Her wells and rivers go dry. Her deserts spread. Her distress plays out in increasingly violent weather patterns. Temperatures rise. Icecaps melt. Oceans acidify. Winds and surf become more violent. Wet places become wetter. Dry places become dryer. Hillsides erode. Forest and prairie fires rage out of control. Coastlands flood. Hillsides become unstable. Her capacity to support life—including human life—declines.

It is not sufficient merely to moderate our reckless behavior to limit the burden we impose on her. We must learn to work with all the members of Earth's community of life to restore her to full health. We must navigate our passage to what Thomas Berry, the cosmologist Brian Swimme, and the spiritual ecologist Mary Evelyn Tucker call the Ecozoic era.

THE ECOZOIC ERA

Berry outlined the underlying frame and implications of an Ecozoic era in an October 1991 lecture sponsored by the E. F. Schumacher Society.[4] These are five critical understandings from that lecture foundational to navigating the turning to a Living Economy for Living Earth.

1. The universe is a communion of subjects, not a collection of objects. Every being has its own inner form, its own spontaneity, its own voice, its ability to declare itself and to be present to other components of the universe in a subject-to-subject relationship.

2. The Earth exists, and can survive, only in its integral functioning. It cannot survive in fragments any more than any organism can survive in fragments.

3. The Earth is a one-time endowment. . . . We must reasonably suppose that the Earth is subject to irreversible damage in the major patterns of its functioning and even to distortions in its possibilities of development.

4. The Earth is primary and humans are derivative. . . . The Earth economy can survive the loss of its human component, but there is no way for the human economy to survive or prosper apart from the Earth economy. . . . The absurdity has been to seek a rising Gross National Product in the face of a declining Gross Earth Product. . . .

   It should be especially clear in medicine that we

cannot have well humans on a sick planet. . . . So in jurisprudence, to poise the entire administration of justice on the rights of humans and their limitless freedom to exploit the natural world is to open the natural world to the worst predatory instincts of humans. The prior rights of the entire Earth community need to be assured first; then the rights and freedoms of humans can have their field of expression.

5. There is no such thing as a human community in any manner separate from the Earth community.

Taking these self-evident truths seriously changes everything.

6 MAKING A LIVING

Scientists debate whether Earth conforms to all the elements of the scientific definition of a living organism. I honor their intellectual rigor and their invaluable contribution to our ever deepening understanding of how life organizes. I am not inclined, however, to wait for science to come to terms with the need to update its definitions.

To participate as productive members of Earth's community of life, we must understand and honor that community's organizing principles and organize our economies accordingly. The principles are universal; the specifics are everywhere unique.

LOCAL SELF-RELIANCE

The biosphere self-organizes as a global system. The locus of intelligent agency, however, is everywhere local and involves trillions of individual choice makers—none of whom is in a position to dominate the rest. This makes possible life's finely tuned micro adaptation to constantly changing local conditions through unimaginably complex processes.

The consequences of local choice making ripple outward

and upward to create global dynamics that ripple back to shape local conditions to which the local community in turn adapts. Yet all the while, Earth as a living superorganism continuously seeks dynamic stability through self-regulating processes we have barely begun to identify, let alone understand—all without evidence of a central decision maker or control mechanism. The dynamics of climate are the most obvious example of this interaction.

Though the system is global, the basic means of sustenance for individual organisms is always local. The imperative is clear. Each community learns to adapt to the distinctive conditions of its place to meet its own needs while engaging in a balanced and mutually beneficial exchange with its neighbors. Each individual species learns to adjust its breeding and consumption accordingly. So long as the local is in balance, so too is the global. It is a brilliant design with clear and unforgiving incentives. Get it right and thrive for the long term. Get it wrong and die.

For so long as the organisms that make up lower-system-level living communities meet their needs in a balanced relationship within the limits of locally available energy, nutrients, and water, so too the higher-level communities up to and including the biosphere are in balance. Natural systems accomplish this coordination without the intervention of a central authority.

MANAGED PERMEABLE BOUNDARIES

At each level of organization—from the individual cell to the multicell organism, to the local eco-community, to the bioregion, to the biosphere—the living organism must define and maintain itself within a managed membrane. This boundary is essential to its ability to maintain its internal flows of energy, nutrients, matter, water, and information in thermodynamic disequilibrium.

Breach the cell wall and the cell's resources dissipate into its environment, resulting in instant death. Death also follows if the exchange between the cell and its environment is blocked. The cell must also have the ability to resist intrusion by toxic substances and by parasites that come to expropriate without corresponding contribution.

The same principle applies at every level of organization. Multicell organisms must have a skin or other protective covering. Oceans, mountains, and climatic zones bound major bioregional communities. Earth's atmosphere serves as a protective membrane within which Living Earth maintains the environmental conditions essential to carbon-based life.

TIME IS LIFE

Life in its natural state self-organizes to make a living in community with joyful exuberance. Premonetization human societies (few of which remain) do the same. When they get it right, there is a natural joy and beauty in life's natural flow as each human member contributes to the cycles of life by which the community sustains itself. Life in both its joys and its sorrows is a continuous flow. There is little distinction between leisure, play, ritual, the work of production, and consumption, and between human and nature. Time is life; life is time.

In societies in a state of advanced monetization, money and global supply chains mediate human access to most all the essentials of living. The system imposes a mandatory sequence of money before life. It segments our lives into disconnected commutes enclosed in steel boxes with wheels between home, work, shopping, school, church, and places of recreation. Our relationships become fragmented, isolated, impersonal, and mediated by money.

Dehumanized and dependent on money to live, we offer ourselves in servitude to money-seeking corporate robots doing work that has no meaning in competition with our co-workers for the favor of a boss who values us only for our contribution to the corporation's bottom line.

There is no depth, no flow, and no time to care. Time is money; money is time. The joy and beauty of making a living and engaging as a contributing member of a living community of life are stripped away. Stripped of our humanity, we increasingly resemble the money-seeking corporate robots we now serve and that mainstream economic theory assumes us to be.

IMAGINE A WORLD . . .

Imagine a world in which we organize ourselves as members of living communities of place. Human-made structures are adapted to their natural settings, support natural processes, and connect people with one another and nature. People meet their needs for energy, nutrients, materials, and information in co-productive partnership with the natural living systems of the place they live. There are no concrete jungles, food deserts, strip malls, or sprawling suburbs. There are gardens everywhere, growing a profuse diversity of beautiful fruits, vegetables, and flowers.

Human settlements organize as self-reliant bioregional food, energy, and water sheds. Major settlements feature a high-population-density car-free urban core designed around public parks, walkways, bicycle paths, and urban gardens. The boundaries of local government jurisdictions coincide with their primary food, energy, and water sheds.

Most people are housed in multifamily, cooperatively owned living units of diverse designs that blend with their landscape clustered around shared facilities: laundries, guest and meeting rooms, composting facilities, solar and geothermal energy heating systems, and office workspaces and support facilities. Neighbors share tools and implements and look out for one another's children at play in car-free commons areas.

Eco-village-style neighborhoods and districts share facilities for the management of nutrients, water, and energy. Many neighborhood and district eco-villages organize as locally owned, self-sustaining economic units offering a variety of locally owned commercial and recreational facilities and investment or employment opportunities reflective of the distinctive tastes, interests, skills, and personal preferences of their residents.

An urban core serves as the bioregion's cultural, educational, and economic hub, providing it with excellent cultural, educational, scientific, and manufacturing facilities.

Each of the region's distinctive eco-villages makes its unique contribution to the diverse, resilient, self-reliant life of the whole.

For eco-villages located in intentionally sparsely populated rural areas, economic activities center on the restoration and sustainable management of soils, forests, and fisheries. Rural eco-villages offer urban visitors opportunities for nature education, recreation, and spiritual practice.

Various forms of public transportation—including car- and ride-share facilities—connect eco-villages to one another and the urban core. Every person has a direct connection to every other person in the world by high-speed Internet and seamless videoconferencing and entertainment facilities.

Most people on most days have no need to venture from the boundaries of the urban core or eco-village in which they live. They meet most mobility needs by walking and biking. Young people are encouraged to take a year to explore the world by foot, train, and ship—connecting to its varied geographies and cultures and building diverse friendships they will maintain throughout their lives through digital communication. Hang-gliding is a favorite sport. Jet air travel is mainly a distant memory.

Money, markets, businesses, and governments are all part of this picture, but they are structured to support balanced and mutually beneficial exchanges within and among communities. People read about the money-seeking corporate robots that once ruled the world and wonder how and why their ancestors tolerated such insanity.

7 ENSLAVED BY CORPORATE ROBOTS

The consolidation of the independent power of corporate robots beyond the control of their CEOs and governing boards is so recent that we are barely beginning to notice its true nature. It is an unintended outcome of a long historical process of increasing human separation from nature and the organization of human societies as hierarchies of imperial domination in which the few control and exploit the many. The nature and implications of the takeover are best understood in historical context.

FROM KINGS TO CORPORATE ROBOTS

Early humans lived in intimate relationship with one another and nature. Our numbers were few, and we fulfilled our essential needs directly from local lands and waters using simple, minimally intrusive technologies. We self-organized as communities to manage our living from local lands and waters, sharing as needed with members of our family and tribe. The earliest trade involved the barter of things that had immediate value, like furs, grain, and cattle.

Somewhere around 3000 BCE there began a turning to imperial rule by kings and priests, who controlled and expropriated the labor and resources of the common people to secure their own power and support extravagant lifestyles. Through the institutions of state and religion, the rulers established a monopoly on the use of armed force to control the means of living (land and water), the instruments of exchange (money and debt), and the cultural stories that legitimated their power.[1]

For thousands of years, imperial rulers expanded their realms by annexing neighboring lands and people. In the 1500s the kings of Europe's most powerful nations—Portugal, Spain, Britain, the Netherlands, Italy, and France—realized that, rather than warring against one another, they better fulfilled their imperial ambitions by colonizing distant territories in Asia, Africa, and the Americas. They often found it convenient to outsource the dirty work to commissioned privateers—that is, state-licensed pirates—some of whom operated powerful naval forces.

By the 1600s, some European monarchs who found their ability to raise and expend revenues constrained by early forms of parliamentary democracy discovered they could earn substantial fees and dividends free from legislative oversight by issuing charters to private investors for limited-liability stockholder-owned corporations. These charters commonly conferred special privileges, including monopoly trading rights for particular goods and regions. Sometimes the issuing sovereign held shares of the companies in their personal accounts. Fielding their own armies and navies, corporations became favored vehicles for colonial domination and exploitation. The British East Indian Company was an early model.

The for-profit publicly traded limited-liability shareholder-owned corporation has proven throughout its history to be an institutional form ideally suited to concentrating economic power under a unified management stripped of human conscience and insulated from accountability for the harms it inflicts on people and nature.

The late twentieth century saw a rapid growth in the size, consolidation, and global reach of corporate power that has continued into the twenty-first century. The most successful corporations absorbed or displaced their competitors, extended their reach far beyond the borders of any state, and shed any credible presumption of commitment to the interests of any place, nation, or peoples.

The global corporation became the favored institution of those who aspire to rule empires beyond the reach of democratic accountability. Then in an ironic twist of fate, something changed.

The public trading of corporate shares in minimally regulated global financial markets became the norm. So too did the aggregation of these shares into funds managed by other profit-seeking corporations devoted to maximizing financial returns by any means. There was a corresponding transition to microsecond computer trading based solely on financial calculations using algorithms that few, if any, humans understand. The result was a near-complete insulation of decision making from the exercise of moral sensibility—even human intention.

It looks as though the divine right of kings has become the divine right of corporate CEOs. In fact, it has become the divine right of capital (money) itself, served and enforced by money-seeking corporate robots that in turn employ managers and other professionals willing to sell their soul for extravagant compensation packages.[2]

DEVELOPMENT AND THE NEW COLONIALISM

Following World War II, national liberation movements dismantled traditional colonialism. Western nations rallied to offer a helping hand to the newly liberated.

In his US presidential inaugural address on January 20, 1949, Harry S. Truman announced his program for "the improvement and growth of underdeveloped areas" as part of a larger effort to end poverty and thereby assure freedom, democracy, and prosperity for all through the expansion of industrial output and trade.

The poor to whom Truman referred as "underdeveloped" were subsistence producers who had no need of money income because they lived directly from local lands and waters without market intervention. By this reckoning, the developed are those who depend on the exchange of money for their means of living—food, shelter, water, education, recreation, and health care. Those in transition from underdeveloped to developed are "developing."

Subsistence producers contribute nothing to the gross domestic product—an indicator of dependence on money and thereby dependence on those who control the creation and allocation of money.

I recall my introduction to development economics in 1959. Economists were explicit. An essential first step on the path to development is to convert subsistence producers to wage labor—migrant agricultural laborers, industrial sweatshop workers, and household help. This "liberates" lands and labor for more "efficient," "higher economic value" use, meaning use that generates profits for those of greater financial means—commonly foreign corporations. Over the years, I came to realize that the preferred development projects frequently support mining, agricultural plantations, factories, dams, roads, shopping malls, golf courses, and vacation resorts—all of which drive the displacement process.

Mining, agricultural, and industrial projects often produce materials for export. Infrastructure projects commonly cater to foreign investors, and resort facilities to foreign tourists. These uses all generate foreign exchange to repay the foreign loans that finance the development projects that drive the displacement. They also finance the import of luxury goods for the wealthy and military arms to repress dissent. Life improves for the few and worsens for the many.

Economists and development agencies point to growth in GDP and money incomes as proof of development success. Mostly the success reduced previously self-reliant peoples to conditions of involuntary servitude to international banks and corporations as their governments ran up massive foreign debts they could not repay.

In 1982, World Bank and International Monetary Fund teams stepped in as debt collectors to impose a menu of "Washington Consensus" structural adjustment policies that included cutting back social programs for the poor, selling public assets and utilities to foreign investors, and opening industries, markets, and natural resources to unrestricted entry and expropriation (legally facilitated theft) by foreign corporations.

The stated goal of the "adjustment" was to repay foreign debts. The deeper consequence was to advance control by money-seeking corporate robots that acknowledge allegiance only to themselves. The recolonized countries of the geographical South thus served as the proving ground for policies that corporate interests subsequently extended to the developed countries of the geographical North through "free" trade agreements.

TAKING THE NEW COLONIALISM GLOBAL

Multilateral agreements like the North American Free Trade Agreement (NAFTA) are favored vehicles to consolidate corporate rule in the geographical North using the same adjustment policies—deregulation, privatization, and the defunding of social programs—used to recolonize the geographical South. The promises are the same: greater economic efficiency, freedom, democracy, and prosperity for all.

Negotiated in secret and quickly pushed through national legislative bodies with minimal review and public debate, these agreements strip national and local governments of their legal power and responsibility to regulate corporate behavior, protect the health and well-being of workers and nature, and manage the flow of money, goods, and services across their borders. Simultaneously, they strengthen corporate rights, particularly intellectual property rights and the presumed right of corporations to sue governments for claimed losses due to regulatory constraints.

Stripped of their protective borders and obligated to secure corporate profits, self-governing democracies are left defenseless against the predatory expropriation of their wealth by corporate robots that have no interest in the well-being of people and nature and over which even national governments no longer have effective control.

The Sacred Money and Markets story's assurance that such policies ultimately work to human benefit grows thin, even as economists continue to assure us that if we just stay the course, it will all work out in the end. One wonders why most economists continue to get it so badly wrong.

IRRATIONAL DELUSIONS OF PHYSICS ENVY

As documented by the science historian Robert Nadeau in *Rebirth of the Sacred: Science, Religion, and the New Environmental Ethos*, the failures of contemporary economics trace back to the mid-1800s to a group of influential economists with a bad case of physics envy.

Physics, then and now, has enjoyed special status as queen of the sciences. The economists in question—Nadeau mentions Stanley Jevons, Léon Walras, Francis Ysidro Edgeworth, and Vilfredo Pareto as leading voices—decided they would elevate economics to the stature of a science on a par with physics by adopting one of its mathematical models.

They chose a model that physicists of the time thought might explain the characteristics of energy in a closed and mechanistic physical system. The economists substituted an ill-defined variable they called utility for energy, assumed in defiance of reality that the economy is a closed and mechanist physical system, and declared economics a science.

Respected scientists and mathematicians pointed out that the economists' adaptation of the model made no logical, scientific, or empirical sense. Physicists eventually concluded that variables in their own version of the model were not measurable and abandoned it.

None of this deterred neoclassical economists, the mainstream of the economics profession. To this day, the adapted model continues to serve as the lens through which economists view the world and to be the basis of their claim that economics is a science.

Nadeau devotes a full chapter to documenting the various ways in which the adapted model is illogical and bears no evident relationship to reality. I highly recommend that anyone who is an economist, aspires to become an economist, or is inclined to look to an economist for economic advice read chapter 7 of *Rebirth of the Sacred*: "The Old

Story: Metaphysics, Mid-Nineteenth Century Physics and Neoclassical Economics."[3]

DEADLY ILLUSIONS

Befuddled and beguiled by the confidence and mathematical voodoo of the current-day intellectual disciples of a group of nineteenth-century economists with an inferiority complex, we bear the consequence of public policies that make sense only in the world of the economists' imagination and pose a serious threat to Living Earth.

In the economists' illusory world:

- There are no material limits to consumption growth.

- Freed from interference by government, ruthless competition in the pursuit of private financial gain leads to a healthy environment and economic prosperity for all.

- Global-scale concentration of monopolistic corporate power maximizes the efficient use of resources for the public benefit.

- Financial markets stripped of human conscience and moral sensibility make resource-allocation decisions more responsive to the needs of people and nature than people make for themselves through their individual and collective choices as democratically self-governing communities.

- The manipulation of financial markets to extract unearned private profits produces real-wealth benefits ultimately shared by all.

The fictions of this illusory world serve grateful economic interests that in turn provide economists with generous support through the foundations, media, think tanks, and educational institutions they fund and control. Economists accept this support as affirmation that their theories generate financial profits for the people who apply them and that they must therefore be valid.

The resulting public policies reduce living communities to dependent nodes in interdependent global supply chains that are inherently fragile, unstable, and prone to collapse as they deplete Living Earth's ability to maintain the conditions essential to life. The many suffer joyless servitude in demeaning jobs in a desperate struggle for survival.

Those for whom there are no jobs turn to crime or simply give up on life. The fortunate few seek solace in ever more extravagant consumption and struggle with money addiction in denial of their meaningless and dehumanizing servitude to computerized financial markets and corporate robots.

That the system compensates the top financiers and corporate managers extravagantly for their services creates an illusory appearance that they are in control. The system, however, is the master. The financiers and CEOs are but pawns of corporate robots they serve but do not control.

Corporate robots are wholly of human creation. Their creators designed them to colonize the labor and resources of the many for the benefit of the few through monopoly control of the means of living. The success of these corporations is so complete that they now function as largely autonomous entities in control of the institutions of government, law, education, and even religion. They now use their control of these institutions to support the final consolidation of their own independent rule.

Although they are entirely of human creation, we had best view and deal with the money-seeking corporate robots as the equivalent of alien invaders. The goal is not to tame them. It is to eliminate them and replace them with institutions accountable to deeply democratic Living Earth communities.

The transition calls for a new economics grounded in a Sacred Life and Living Earth story.

8 A NEW ECONOMICS FOR A NEW ECONOMY

The only valid purpose of an economy is to serve life. To align the human economy with this purpose, we must learn to live as nature lives, organize as nature organizes, and learn as nature learns guided by a reality-based, life-centered, intellectually sound economics that embraces the values and insights of the Sacred Life and Living Earth story.

The quest for a new economics begins with a simple question for which the answer should be obvious: Is the purpose of the economy to maximize the profits of money-seeking corporate robots or the health and well-being of living households?

BEGIN WITH THE HOUSEHOLD

One of the most important single contributions to my understanding of where mainstream economics went wrong came from Sixto Roxas, an economist and former international bank executive. We became close friends and colleagues when I lived in the Philippines in the 1980s. I once asked him, "Why do economists so often come up with the wrong answers?"

Without a moment's hesitation, he responded, "Because they chose the firm rather than the household as the basic unit of analysis. Economists view the economy as an aggregation of profit-seeking firms rather than an aggregation of living households."[1]

To illustrate the implications, he noted that the firm seeks to hire as few workers as possible at the lowest possible wage. The household wants to find jobs for all its job seekers at the highest possible wage.

He then offered an example related to nature. A community of households has a natural interest in a healthy local forest as a sustained source of its essential means of living. It provides beauty, a place to hike and camp, a supply of building materials and firewood, freshwater from its streams and aquifers, roots that stabilize the soils of a steep hillside, a filter that cleanses the air of dust and impurities.

For an international timber corporation, the local forest is a commodity to harvest and sell for a onetime profit on its way to the next forest. The fewer workers required, the shorter the term of their employment, and the lower their pay, the better.

Whether we conclude that clear-cutting the forest produces a net economic benefit or a net economic loss depends on whether we take the Sacred Money and Markets perspective of a money-seeking global corporation or the Sacred Life and Living Earth perspective of a life-seeking local household.

The distinction between firm and household becomes most salient when the dominant firms are placeless money-seeking corporate robots captive to the demands of global financial markets that value only money. The distinction is less consequential in an economy organized around locally owned family or cooperatively owned businesses that function as extensions of the local households that own and staff them.

VEST POWER IN LIVING PEOPLE

If we choose an economy that favors the interests of living households and communities, we will structure its institutions to:

1. Root power in local households and communities through local ownership and local decision making.

2. Foster local diversity and self-reliance in securing a means of living for all the community's members using local energy, nutrients, water, and material resources.

3. Cultivate and reward civic engagement, responsibility, the sharing of work and resources (including a free exchange of ideas, knowledge, and information), and honest dealing in the interest of the well-being of all.

4. Encourage everyone to contribute according to their ability, and recognize the right of each to meet their reasonable needs with due consideration for the needs of others.

5. Maintain permeable managed boundaries as necessary

to the integrity of the community, support fair and balanced trade of local surplus with neighbors, and secure the community's resources against theft by intruding predators.

Such measures root economic power in living households and communities and help focus the attention of both households and firms on the creation of real living wealth rather than phantom financial wealth.

PHANTOM-WEALTH ECONOMICS

We are conditioned by the Sacred Money and Markets story to equate money with wealth and the making of money with wealth creation. As previously noted, money is only a number, an accounting chit, a potential claim against things of real value. Money itself has value only because by social convention we accept it for things of real value.

Money created through the manipulation of financial markets unrelated to creating anything of real value is phantom wealth—a baseless and generally unjust claim against society's real wealth. Wall Street daily demonstrates its ability to create phantom financial wealth in massive sums.

Mainstream Sacred Money and Markets economics is a phantom-wealth economics for which money is the defining value and making money by any means is the defining purpose. Phantom-wealth economics values people and nature (living wealth) only as commodified resources based on their market price. Thus, it assigns breathable air no value, though we can live without it for only a few minutes. It assigns diamonds a very high value, though we easily live without them.

Picture yourself alone on a desert island with nothing to sustain you. As your ship sank, you had to choose between two trunks. One trunk is filled with emergency supplies and rations—market value maybe a couple hundred dollars. The other is full of hundred-dollar bills totaling maybe a million dollars. Schooled in the Sacred Money and Markets story, you went for the million dollars. Oops.

Acting on the advice of economists suffering from physics envy, we manage our affairs to maximize stocks (financial assets) and flows (GDP) of money (accounting units). We neglect the care of the living systems on which our existence and well-being depend because by the logic of phantom-wealth economics, it isn't profitable.

The language of phantom-wealth economics actively hides the critical distinction between phantom (money) wealth and real (living) wealth. Within the Sacred Money and Markets frame, most conversations about the economy feature constant references to assets, capital, resources, and wealth. None of these terms distinguishes phantom financial wealth from real living wealth.[2]

By the logic of Sacred Money and Markets economics, there is no need to distinguish between phantom financial wealth and real living wealth because all forms of capital ultimately translate into money equivalents on a balance sheet. Since, in theory, any asset with a market value can be exchanged for any other of equivalent market value, the specific form of the capital, resource, asset, or wealth is of no particular importance. For profit-maximizing corporations, this logic has some validity. For a society, it leads to significant distortion.

For example, the world's total financial assets significantly exceed the market value of the world's real wealth. This creates expectations of entitlement by those who hold these financial assets that can never be realized and leads financial commentators to confuse stock and housing price bubbles with wealth creation.

This confusion is a particular issue for the US Federal Reserve, for which a rising wage is inflationary and a rising asset price is wealth creation. It thus manages the money supply to hold down wages and inflate asset prices—a certain formula for growing inequality and driving financial boom and bust.

For years, I puzzled when I heard commentators speak solemnly of "international capital movements." I imagined huge ships transporting machine tools, construction equipment, and other instruments of production from one country to another. Eventually, I learned that international capital movements that sometimes throw national economies into wild gyrations mostly involve nothing more than a bank transferring numbers from one account to another—quite possibly within the same computer—in response to financial speculators.

Focused on caring for money, we neglect everything that is essential to our well-being. Using conventional economic analysis, we manage the economy to maximize financial returns to money, as if money were the primary resource constraint—rather than, say, water, fertile land, or skilled workers. Consequently, we believe we are getting richer as a society when every living system essential to our well-being is in distress from our abuse and neglect.

In fact, money is the most easily created of all the many forms of what we call capital. Any central bank can create it in an instant in any needed amount with little more than a computer keystroke. For a country with a central bank, unmet needs, and underutilized real resources, money should never be the defining constraint.

Money, markets, and corporations can all be useful servants. They are terrible masters. We are in desperate need of a living-wealth economics to guide our way to restoring money, markets, and corporations to their proper servant role.

LIVING-WEALTH ECONOMICS

Within the frame of a living-wealth economics, nature is our source of life and is therefore precious beyond price. The ultimate measure of the economy's performance is the health and vitality of Earth's living systems and the living beings (including humans) they comprise. The healthier and more productive Living Earth's generative systems, the greater her ability to meet our human needs and those of all of Earth's community's countless other living beings in perpetuity. A living-wealth economics will therefore give top priority to assuring that we allocate our life energy in ways that optimize the health of Living Earth's generative systems.

Embracing the Sacred Life and Living Earth story frame, a living-wealth economics will recognize that we belong to Earth; Earth does not belong to us. It will guide us to an economy in which we meet our human needs through our active participation in, and positive contribution to, the ecosystem processes by which the microbes, plants, animals, and geological structures of Living Earth maintain and renew freshwater supplies, the chemical composition of sea and air, air pressure, surface temperature, climate stability, soil fertility, fisheries, forests, and grasslands to sustain the conditions essential to Earth life.

A living-wealth economics will focus not on how best to allocate money to maximize financial returns, but rather how best to allocate our life energy—essentially human time and talent—to maximize living returns to people and nature. It will honor life's inherent wisdom as expressed through Earth's natural living systems. It will guide us in learning from, working with, facilitating, and assisting and augmenting Earth's natural processes.

A living-wealth economics will give particular priority to guiding our management of human, social, intellectual, and physical infrastructure capital. These are all of distinctive human origin and represent our human capacity to enhance the quality of living for all people and contribute to maintaining the living systems essential to all Earth life and to advancing life's creative evolutionary unfolding.

Each form of human-created capital requires a continuing investment of our life energy in their maintenance and renewal. A living community stands to reap major living returns from such investments. Rarely is there a financial incentive for an individual for-profit firm to make such investments in the absence of government intervention to require or subsidize it.

To create and maintain human capital requires us to invest human time and talent in educating ourselves, developing job skills, and meeting the requirements of healthy living, including exercise and continuous flows of nutritious food, clean air and water, and health care. To create and maintain social capital requires us to invest human time and talent in social interactions, ritual, and artistic expression to build and maintain trust and a sense of common purpose and identity. To create and maintain intellectual capital requires us to invest human time and talent in research, documentation, sharing, and updating. To create and maintain physical infrastructure capital requires us to invest human time and talent in design, construction, and maintenance.

All these forms of human-created capital are interrelated. Each involves constant interaction with the living systems of nature.

A phantom-wealth economics embraces and promotes the Sacred Money and Markets story to legitimate and grow the power of money-seeking corporate robots. A living-wealth economics embraces and promotes the Sacred Life and Living Earth story to legitimate and affirm the right and capacity of life-seeking people to self-organize as living households and communities. As we reclaim the story space that the corporate robots have co-opted, we reclaim both our power and our humanity.

9 A LIVING ECONOMY FOR A LIVING EARTH

If we get our story right, we can get our institutions right. If we get our institutions right, we get our future right.

Institutions based on the design principles of the Sacred Money and Markets story empower computer-driven financial markets and corporate robots to base society's major resource-allocation decisions solely on the logic of short-term financial returns.

Institutions based on the design principles of a Sacred Life and Living Earth story empower living people to make these decisions as responsible members of living households and communities based on long-term living returns.

Here are some examples of critical institutional design choices.

PERFORMANCE INDICATORS

When we organize by the Sacred Money and Markets story, we use growth in financial metrics like the gross domestic product (GDP), corporate profits, and stock prices as the basis for assessing economic performance and making policy decisions. We thus focus on optimizing the economy's service to money.

GDP counts everything exchanged for money as an economic benefit, even if it results in the destruction of fisheries and forests, and the poisoning of rivers and aquifers. Expenditures related to divorce, toxics cleanup, and the treatment of cancer and mental illness—along with financial-sector income from activities that produce no real value and much else that may generate short-term profits for business at great cost to society—all count as a positive economic benefit.

By the Sacred Money and Markets story reckoning, population growth is an economic benefit because it grows consumption, business profits, the demand for jobs, and GDP even as it creates ever more intolerable pressure on Earth's living systems. Replacing the home production of food and childcare with purchased food and childcare grows GDP.

GDP is a decidedly mixed bag. The faster we monetize relationships, breed, increase our dependence on the financial oligarchy, and advance toward social and environmental collapse, the faster the GDP and share price indexes grow. Benefits are short-term and illusory. Costs are long-term—and for our species, potentially terminal.

When we organize by the Sacred Life and Living Earth story, we focus on improving the health of people, community, and Living Earth. This requires more than different metrics; it requires a different mindset.

A politician going to an economist to ask, "What policies will accelerate US GDP growth?" is like a person with an overweight, misshapen, cancer-ridden body asking a doctor, "What can I do to gain weight?" With very rare exception, rapid adult weight gain is a warning sign of significant mental or physical dysfunction.

To assess how well the economy is serving living people, we properly look to indicators of life satisfaction, nutritional health, creative expression, freedom from chronic disease and psychological dysfunction, the frequency and quality of interactions with people and nature, the sense of contribution, and the allocation of time between activities that bring intrinsic satisfaction versus those we simply endure to make money. The most powerful indicators of healthy community function are indicators of the health and well-being of our children. For Living Earth, we look at indicators of biodiversity, climate stability, the health of rivers and aquifers, and the health of bee, frog, and fish populations.

Given the complex nuances of healthy living systems, selecting specific indicators merits extended public conversation and the attention of our best minds.

To continue the medical analogy, a living-wealth economist will act in the manner of a naturopathic physician who looks at many indicators of bodily function for clues to the source of systemic failures in the body's self-managed healing and health maintenance processes. Rather than directly treat the symptoms of system failure, he or she will recommend actions to address the cause of the symptoms.

For example, in the United States, one of our most telling indicators of profound social and economic system failure is the proportion of our adult population in prison. We could immediately move that indicator in a positive direction simply by releasing large numbers of the incarcerated back to the general population. That, however, would do nothing to resolve the variety of economic system failures that create the extreme inequality and critical shortage of living-wage jobs that in turn result in broken overstressed homes and push excluded people into drug consumption, drug dealing, and other crimes.[1]

The ecological economist Joshua Farley suggests we view GDP as an indicator of the economic cost of producing a given level of well-being. We might then manage the economy to minimize, rather than maximize, cost.

Perhaps our best indication that we are making meaningful progress in the turning to a living future will be when our national accounts report a simultaneous improvement in the well-being of life (economic benefit) and a decline in GDP (economic cost).

LEGAL RIGHTS AND RESPONSIBILITIES

Modern nations profess a nearly universal commitment to democracy and human rights, including the right to life, liberty, and the pursuit of happiness.

Yet legal practice directly contradicts this commitment in troubling ways. It prioritizes the rights of private for-profit corporations over the human rights of living persons and holds corporations to a lower standard of accountability than living persons for harms against society. It gives nature no rights at all.

Money Economy advocates push aggressively for US Supreme Court decisions and multilateral trade agreements that strengthen the rights of corporate robots, weaken the rights of living people and communities, and strip nature of any protection whatever. Such measures, they argue, are essential to maintain and accelerate economic growth. By the values and understanding of the Sacred Money and Markets story, this makes sense.

By the values and understanding of the Sacred Life and Living Earth story, prioritizing the rights of corporate robots over the rights of living people and nature to accelerate the monetization of relationships and grow the financial assets of the already rich is not only illogical but actively and insanely suicidal.

Without nature, there are no people. Without people, there are no corporations, there is no property, and there is no money. The rights of nature logically take priority. Indeed, there is a strong argument that the most foundational of human rights is the right to a healthy environment. By extension we have both the right and the responsibility to secure and defend the rights of nature. Our existence and well-being depend on her.

A corporation is created when the government issues a charter. There is no reason for any corporation to exist other than to serve a democratically determined public interest. It is odd, indeed, when the law grants a rogue corporate robot rights that trump the rights of the living community that created it.

Essential political action will establish in law that:

- Natural rights are exclusive to living beings, including Living Earth.

- Because the health and integrity of Living Earth is essential to the right of current and future human generations to life, liberty, and the pursuit of happiness, the right to protect her health and integrity is the most basic of human rights.

- Exercise of the right to protect Living Earth's health and integrity is the most basic of human responsibilities.

OWNERSHIP, WORK, AND LIVELIHOODS

Ownership is power. When that power resides in global financial markets and corporations, it supports making money. When distributed among living people in living communities, it supports making a living.

Here we confront another consequence of a legal system that gives the right of corporations to make a profit priority over the right of people to make a living. By current legal practice, there is no practical limit to the right of a corporation to monopolize the ownership of land, water, seeds, energy, health care facilities, educational facilities, and other essentials of life to extract unearned monopoly profits. The greater their profits, the greater their ability to consolidate monopoly control of the means of living to extort ever larger monopoly rents.

When ownership secures a person's right to a basic means of living, it secures that person against the tyranny of dependence on money and those who control money's creation and allocation. When ownership secures the right of a person or corporation to monopolize the means of living and then to profit from the desperation of those deprived, it becomes an instrument of tyranny rather than a defense against it.

Living Earth is the creation and common heritage of all of Earth's living beings. The idea that it is the right of a few humans to own it to the exclusion of all others is a moral travesty. The idea that it is the right of nonliving money-seeking robots to own it to the exclusion of humans—and even to destroy, contaminate, or otherwise render it useless or hazardous to future generations—is a logical, as well as a moral, travesty.

A living economy is composed of and served by living enterprises owned by living people who depend on them for their livelihood. Known to the other members of the community in which they live, these owners have a strong incentive to act with conscience and moral sensibility.[2] It is for good reason that Adam Smith and Thomas Jefferson favored economies based on small firms and farms owned by individuals and families with a sense of loyalty to their place and their neighbors.

Private ownership by individuals or households of the means of creating their living consistent with their reasonable needs aligns household and enterprise interests. It is an essential foundation of both democracy and socially efficient markets. It provides a bulwark against the tyranny of a monopolization of property rights whether by individuals, corporations, or states.

Many economic functions in modern society do require larger enterprise units, even within a Living Economy framework. We can meet this need in ways consistent with broad, equitable, stable, and locally rooted participation in ownership through cooperative ownership structures, of which we have many examples.[3]

The worker-owned Mondragón cooperatives in Spain are a leading example of the application of the principles of co-operative worker ownership in a large, complex enterprise.

FINANCIAL SERVICES

The power to create and allocate money is the ultimate power in any society in which access to a basic means of living depends on money. When money-seeking corporate robots exercise this power in secret, free from democratic account-ability, it becomes the ultimate instrument of tyranny.

The tyranny will prevail for so long as we accept the story that money is wealth, making money is the economy's de-fining purpose, and the profits of a business define its value to society. Within this story frame, the megascale financial institutions that reap outsize profits from speculation and the sophisticated manipulation of financial markets merit respect and deference as society's most productive wealth creators—even though they produce nothing of value, create financial instability, and drive increasingly unjust inequality.

The reality-based Sacred Life and Living Earth story exposes the essential truth: Money is an accounting token.

Money and a modest monetary profit are means, not ends. Institutions, including financial *services* institutions, are properly valued for their contribution to the health and vitality of the communities they serve. By this standard, Wall Street financial institutions are a net societal liability.

The United States created a decentralized, community-rooted banking system in response to the financial crash of 1929. This well-proven financial services system model financed the United States' victory in World War II, produced an unprecedented period of economic stability and prosperity, made America the world's leading industrial power, financed major national investments in infrastructure, created the American middle class, made America the world's leading creditor nation, and put a man on the moon. Then Wall Street stepped in, dismantled it, and put in place a system devoted largely to speculation and the gaming of global financial markets.

Beginning in the 1970s, Wall Street used its political power to push through financial deregulation and consolidate the financial sector under control of its megabanks, hedge funds, and private equity funds. The resulting Wall Street system acted like a vacuum cleaner, sucking money out of local communities where it might have supported productive exchange and investment. It flowed instead to Wall Street financial institutions engaged in financial gaming to generate management bonuses and unearned profits for the most wealthy.

We bear the devastating consequences. The United States is now neither an industrial power nor a middle-class nation.

We have become the world's leading debtor nation, suffered a major financial collapse in 2008 followed by continuing economic stagnation and high unemployment, and now face the near certainty of an even more devastating financial collapse in the near future.

In a Living Economy, banks and other financial sector institutions are creations of the living communities they serve. Human-scale, cooperatively owned, locally rooted, and accountable, they give living communities the ability to create credit in official currency in response to local needs and opportunities through processes that are transparent and democratically accountable. Money—including profits and interest—circulate locally.[4] Individuals rotate between roles as owners and workers, borrowers and lenders. Some may have a bit more, some a bit less—but without clear class divisions. Money is servant. Life is master.

We have the right and the means as democratic societies to restore sensible financial rules and create a financial system based on these same principles.

GOVERNANCE

By the reckoning of the Sacred Money and Markets story, the primary—if not sole—legitimate purpose of government is to maintain essential order, enforce contracts, and secure property rights, all of which serve money-seeking corporate robots. Beyond these functions, corporate interests expect government to leave the free market to its own devices.

This ignores an inherent paradox. In a free (unregulated) market, successful corporations grow. The bigger they get, the greater their monopoly power and their ability and temptation to abuse that power. The greater the abuse, the greater the need for big government to restrain the abuse, come to the aid of the abused, and clean up the environmental mess. The best way to reduce the size of government is to reduce the size of corporations.

The bigger the corporation, however, the greater its political power and thereby its ability to resist regulation and avoid paying the taxes required to enforce the regulations and to fund the social and environmental programs that corporate abuse makes necessary. In the worst-case scenario—as we now experience—big corporations co-opt big government to extract subsidies, protect monopolies, and shift the tax burden from the rich to the poor.

Within the Sacred Life and Living Earth story frame, we make public policy based on what helps people and nature self-organize locally as healthy living communities within an essential framework of appropriate rules, government fiscal policy, and public facilities. Appropriate rules include restrictions on the size of individual firms in order to maintain market discipline and prevent the concentration of monopoly power.

There is no place in a Living Economy for unregulated money-seeking publicly traded limited-liability corporate robots. They must be broken up and restructured to function as human-scale, cooperatively owned, community-rooted enterprises.

Democratic governments of we the people have an essential role: to create and maintain a framework of rules and institutions that keep markets fair and support our self-organization as responsible contributing members of the local eco-communities that are the source of our living. This governmental responsibility is equivalent to my responsibility to my body to maintain the conditions essential to the processes of its constituent cells to self-organize to maintain my living function.

The proper governmental regulatory, public finance, and fiscal policy priorities in a Living Economy society seek to:

- Secure the access of all households to a means of creating their own living though some combination of paid employment, self-production, and community labor sharing.

- Shift employment away from activities that harm society to activities that benefit society.

- Assure that the benefits of productivity gains are shared by owners and workers and distributed between increased income and increased free time to improve the work-home balance.

- Support equitable and democratic participation in ownership and fair market exchange.

- Make unproductive financial speculation unprofitable.

- Create economic incentives that favor locally rooted and accountable businesses over footloose corporate robots.

ACADEMIA

Shaped by the pressures of the Money Economy, our academic institutions have become factories for producing compliant debt-burdened workers for indentured service to corporate robots. The values and assumptions of the Sacred Money and Markets story permeate their structures, cultures, and curricula. Their economics departments and schools of business and public policy are well funded and staffed to promote the morally and intellectually corrupt story as science.

Rare is the university that has a single course, even in departments of philosophy or schools of theology, devoted to exploring the power of the stories by which we define ourselves, the stories that shaped our historical past, the need for a new story for our time, and the sources from which such a story might draw.

We have an urgent need for leaders with the skills and understanding required to advance our turning to a Living Economy. Rather than indoctrination in the fallacies of the Sacred Money and Markets story, they need schooling in the values and understanding of the Sacred Life and Living Earth story. They need skills in observing, understanding, and adapting human institutions to the living systems of Living Earth within the frame of a living-wealth economics.

Academic institutions organized by narrowly defined siloed disciplines that organize knowledge within the limited frame of the Grand Machine cosmology are poorly suited to this need.

One can learn a great deal about the inner workings of a machine by carefully disassembling it, studying the parts individually, and then reassembling them to restore the mechanism to its original state.

To disassemble a living being is to kill it and thereby destroy its essence. To fragment knowledge is to suppress our natural ability to perceive and relate to Earth as a living being.

The complex, active, and interdependent processes by which life maintains the conditions of its own existence involve a combination of mechanism, chance, and conscious agency. To live consciously as contributing members of Earth's community of life, we must understand the nature and interplay of all three. Most science education ignores, even denies, the existence of the third and most important—conscious agency.

Schools of business, public policy, engineering, architecture, and urban planning face a particular challenge. We need decision makers in all these fields skilled in creating and managing the institutional and physical infrastructure of a society in which life is the goal, money and markets are means, and the built environment reconnects us with one another and nature.

The physical walls that isolate learning from life worsen the problem of the intellectual walls that isolate disciplines from one another. We come to truly understand life only through active, disciplined, observant engagement in living.

Most of the learning relevant to our turning from a Money Economy to a Living Economy is taking place outside the walls of academia. Those who lead the way exhibit a deep love of life and possess the wisdom of the heart. Some may have advanced academic credentials; most do not.

They share their learning through blogs, web publications, workshops, and conferences. Learning accumulates in the cultural and social DNA of the communities in which it occurs. There is a great need for systematic documentation to facilitate sharing and thereby accelerate humanity's global learning process.

The continued relevance of today's educational institutions depends on their willingness and ability to rethink, retool, and restructure as they learn to connect with and serve the grassroots social-learning initiatives taking place all around them. They need to:

- Strip away the intellectual walls that isolate academic disciplines from one another and the physical walls that isolate formal learning from the living world.

- Organize faculty and students into interdisciplinary learning teams that reach out to, engage, support, and learn from nearby community-based social-learning initiatives.

- Shift their focus from specialized pre-employment degree programs to facilitation of lifelong learning.

- Replace the metaphor of the machine with the metaphor of the living organism as the defining intellectual frame.

- Staff departments of biology and ecology with biologists and ecologists who view life through a living-systems lens.

- Feature history courses that examine through a holistic system lens how large-scale social transformation has occurred in human societies and draw out relevant lessons for contemporary change agents.

- Replace economics departments with departments of living-household ecology and management that are staffed by applied ecologists. Confine the teaching of neoclassical economics to courses seeking lessons from a variety of historical examples of self-destructive intellectual misadventures.

- Replace a business and public policy curriculum designed around the values and logic of phantom-wealth economics with one designed around the values and logic of living-wealth economics.

- Replace engineering, architecture, and urban planning curricula centered on creating an auto-oriented infrastructure that suppresses nature and walls us off from life with curricula that support creating a life-oriented built infrastructure that connects us with one another and nature as living members of a living community.

- Introduce law school courses exploring the nature, structure, and doctrines of an Earth law/rights of nature legal system.

FROM POLITICALLY INFEASIBLE TO POLITICALLY INEVITABLE

Navigating a turning from the story and institutions of a Money Economy to those of a Living Economy presents a daunting challenge. Given the accelerating rates of environmental and social collapse, time is short.

No compromise is possible between the values and power structures of Money Economy and Living Economy systems. Their differences are irreconcilable. There is no way to produce outsize financial returns to the assets of billionaires, allow the few to monopolize the control of and disrupt Earth's living systems for a quick profit, and simultaneously maintain the conditions essential to Earth life and meet the needs of all.

We cannot get to a just, sustainable, and peaceful world with reforms that tweak the existing system at its margins. Each of the system changes outlined above is essential.

The politically pragmatic observer will point out that these may be good ideas, but given the power of the pro-growth, pro-trade, relationship-monetizing, monopoly-creating, money-seeking, corporate-robot-serving establishment, they are not politically feasible. True.

If, however, we limit ourselves to what is politically feasible, we in effect declare that human survival is politically infeasible. That creates a self-fulfilling prophecy and assures we will end up where we are going.

The only intelligent course is to define together what is necessary. Then together we'll figure out how we will make it politically inevitable. Transformation can—and does—occur even in the face of determined repression by powerful interests that control mass media, education, and state power.

I have witnessed in my lifetime a number of politically

infeasible transformations. These include the collapse of British rule in India, the transformation of race relations and gender roles, the fall of the Berlin Wall and the disintegration of the Soviet Union, the end of apartheid in South Africa, and the ouster of the Marcos dictatorship in the Philippines. Each seemed impossible—until it happened. Then suddenly it seemed inevitable. Each helped to prepare the way for the work now at hand.

When a moment of readiness arises, a breakthrough can occur with surprising speed as a new public consensus forms.

The key is the story. We will not achieve the system changes outlined above through direct political confrontation with the institutions of the Money Economy. Far better are our prospects for changing the story that legitimates their power. Everything else then follows.

10 OWN THE STORY, OWN THE FUTURE

We humans organize around stories. Whoever owns a society's defining story owns its future. Corporate robots and their minions relentlessly promote the Sacred Money and Markets story as the defining frame for every policy debate in which they have an interest. They have made their story the defining story of what is now a global society.

Popular movements dedicated to advancing democracy, racial and gender equality, environmental health, and peace organize around discrete issues. They frame their arguments either in terms of values they hold to be self-evident or within the frame of the Sacred Money and Markets story. They thus concede the story frame and thereby the future.

For so long as the Sacred Money and Markets story remains the uncontested framing story of the public culture, we view the world through the lens of money. We see money, think money, and live in service to money. Money owns our future.

When we view the same reality through the lens of life, we see life, think life, and live in service to life. Our living future should not, need not, be lost for the lack of an authentic story that acknowledges the self-evident truth that we are living beings for whom life comes before money.

The Sacred Money and Markets story is rapidly losing its public credibility as awareness spreads that it rests on a foundation of bad ethics, bad science, and bad economics. To discredit a corrupt story, however, is not sufficient. It must be replaced by a more credible and compelling story.

LIVING THE FUTURE

Ever larger numbers of thoughtful people are walking away from the idolatrous money story and the institutions it serves. They organize to live in co-productive community with one another and nature in ways that support their own and nature's self-healing.

The leadership, learning, and decision making for this work are—and must be—in the hands of local people motivated by a concern for the health, resilience, and sustained well-being of the communities in which they live. They share lessons, experience, and inspiration freely via the Internet. They build communities of place that reduce dependence on money, increase local control and self-determination, and advance democracy as a way of life.

In each such initiative, participants redirect their life energy from the institutions of the dying extractive Money Economy to the institutions of the emerging generative Living Economy. As the Living Economy gains in scale and visibility, it provides a growing range of attractive opportunities for employment, shopping, and investment for others inclined to join in the cause of life.

They establish family farms and farmers' markets and promote urban agriculture to rebuild local food systems. They revive rites of passage that reconnect generations to one another and to forces of life seen and unseen. They establish and patronize locally owned human-scale businesses that rebuild local ownership, self-reliance, and self-determination. They work with local governments to create bicycle-friendly streets, incorporate living-building standards into building codes, create zero-waste local recycling systems, install wind- and solar-energy generation, create and move their money to local banks and credit unions. They promote cooperative ownership and introduce indicator systems by which people can assess local economic performance against indicators of the health of people, community, and nature.[1]

Architects, builders, and urban planners create living buildings, neighborhoods, communities, and cities. Young and old come together to create eco-villages that bear resemblance to traditional extended family households and organize to produce a portion of their own sustenance to reduce their dependence on money and markets. Social entrepreneurs organize car and bicycle sharing.

Communities organize to manage nearby forest ecosystems to restore and maintain forest health and provide livelihood opportunities for local people. Young people return to the land and learn to live from farming and ranching using methods that support the regeneration of soils and aquifers.

The physical encampments of the Occupy movement served as social laboratories in which a new generation explored the processes and possibilities of radical self-organization in community without money or centralizing governance structures.

Many initiatives involve local businesses, nonprofits, associations, or cooperatives. Some involve only informal arrangements among friends and neighbors. There may be monetary exchange, but profit is rarely the driver.

The more sophisticated organizations are asking, "Does our work merely provide temporary relief for a few victims of a failed system, or does it make an incremental contribution to shifting power from Money Economy values and institutions to Living Economy values and institutions?" National People's Action is a leading example.[2]

Rather than provide temporary shelter for the homeless, such organizations work with local governments to exercise eminent domain and recover homes illegally foreclosed by Wall Street banks and return them to their proper owners or get them into the hands of the otherwise homeless to turn the homeless into homeowners. Rather than establish a new soup kitchen, they create cooperative community gardens on rooftops and vacant lots for the jobless and underpaid to grow their own food with pride and dignity and reconnect with one another and nature. Each time an otherwise dependent and excluded person begins to gain control over their means of basic living there is a modest but incremental shift in power that contributes to a new frame of possibility.

Individually, most such actions fall short of actual system change, but they contribute to a new frame for system-scale initiatives with the potential to create supportive system-level rule changes.

At the system level, rather than seek marginal regulatory restraints on the destructive practices of predatory megabanks, such organizations campaign to break them up and convert them into community banks cooperatively owned by the people who depend on them for financial services—an example of deep power-shifting system transformation.

A MOVEMENT OF MOVEMENTS

Close up, these individual efforts seem scattered, marginal, even naive in the face of the corporate power they dare to challenge.

Step back, however, and we discern the outlines of an emerging interracial, intercultural global-scale social movement—an inclusive intersectoral movement of movements—converging on a trajectory toward a Living Earth future. Lacking a name and a unifying story, this movement of movements remains invisible to the broader public, the institutional robots of the Money Economy it seeks to displace, and even to itself.

Yet at every hand, this movement challenges the power and legitimacy of the Money Economy's corporate robots as it surrounds them and occasionally infiltrates them to recruit allies from the ranks of the mercenaries and indentured servants in their employ.

Imperial rulers, whether king or corporate robot, depend on the obedience of the ruled. Their seemingly invincible power is an illusion. They hold only the power that the people yield to them. When people walk away from their corporate masters to rebuild their lives and communities, they reclaim for themselves and their community their labor, ingenuity, resources, and vision.

When the people of the original thirteen British colonies of North America chose to walk away from the British king, they did not seek a more benevolent king. They sought an end to monarchy in favor of democracy. Those who walk away from servitude to corporate robots seek an end to corporate rule in favor of living self-governing democracies of people and nature.

We already have enormous momentum in the many millions of people who at some level recognize the failure of the old story. These people are mobilizing to resist further corporate destruction of life as they live into being the culture and institutions of a living future.

Each initiative contributes to a growing momentum for change. To become a truly transformative force, however, the emerging movement needs a shared public story—one that connects and frames the movement's varied elements and the vision of possibility that together we have the potential to make real. A compelling and broadly inclusive story of possibility is the key to building the movement's visibility and coherence.

A STORY OF THE GRANDEST OF ALL EPIC JOURNEYS

In its full expression, the Sacred Life and Living Earth story is an inspiring tale of the human place in the grandest of all epic journeys, the journey of an evolving Living Universe. The story draws from many sources of human knowledge and understanding to give deep meaning to our existence. It exposes the myopic banality of the Sacred Money and Markets story. It offers an appealing vision of human possibility. And it provides a frame for practical action.

It joins three narratives, each of which underscores the significance of life's extraordinary interdependence and capacity to self-organize to advance the interests of the whole in fulfillment of a profound cosmic purpose. Each of these narratives is gaining form and clarity through what so far have been largely independent conversations.

Narrative 1: The Living Universe

The Living Universe narrative recognizes and celebrates the unity of all being. It connects the domains of science and religion and draws from the breadth and depth of human experience and knowledge. It reveals the wonder and complexity of the creative, self-organizing processes by which the universe unfolds toward ever greater complexity, beauty, awareness, and possibility.

Respected scientists write popular books about consciousness, intelligence, and the need to move beyond material reductionism in science. Leading spiritual thinkers write books and articles on sacred activism connecting the insights of spiritual and scientific inquiry. Interfaith conversations move beyond seeking mutual religious tolerance to acknowledge, honor, and synthesize the contributions of diverse spiritual traditions with the contributions of science.

The emerging synthesis draws from the Distant Patriarch cosmology the insight that there is agency and purpose in creation. It draws from the Grand Machine cosmology the insight that there is order and chance in creation. It draws from the Mystical Unity cosmology the insight that matter is a mental construct, consciousness is the unifying ground of creation, we are all connected, and ego can be a barrier to enlightenment without a disciplined alignment with cosmic purpose.

Narrative 2: Living Earth

The Living Earth narrative honors Earth as a creative, adapting, resilient, evolving, self-organizing community of life and the birth mother of our species. It acknowledges our dependence on and responsibility to contribute to the adaptive, resilient processes by which Earth's community of life captures, processes, and shares energy, nutrients, water, and information to maintain and enhance the conditions of Earth life.

Elements of the Living Earth narrative are finding their way into international and local forums. With leadership from indigenous communities, civil society groups produced a Universal Declaration of the Rights of Mother Earth at the World People's Conference on Climate Change and the Rights of Mother Earth in Cochabamba, Bolivia, in 2010. It includes an eloquent statement affirming Earth as a living being. (See "Universal Declaration of Rights of Mother Earth.")

UNIVERSAL DECLARATION
OF RIGHTS OF MOTHER EARTH

World People's Conference on Climate Change
and the Rights of Mother Earth, Cochabamba, Bolivia,
April 22, 2010

ARTICLE 1. MOTHER EARTH

1. Mother Earth is a living being.

2. Mother Earth is a unique, indivisible, self-regulating community of interrelated beings that sustains, contains and reproduces all beings.

3. Each being is defined by its relationships as an integral part of Mother Earth.

4. The inherent rights of Mother Earth are inalienable in that they arise from the same source as existence.

5. Mother Earth and all beings are entitled to all the inherent rights recognized in this Declaration without distinction of any kind, such as may be made between organic and inorganic beings, species, origin, use to human beings, or any other status.

6. Just as human beings have human rights, all other beings also have rights which are specific to their species or kind and appropriate for their role and function within the communities within which they exist.

7. The rights of each being are limited by the rights of other beings and any conflict between their rights must be resolved in a way that maintains the integrity, balance and health of Mother Earth.

SOURCE: http://therightsofnature.org/universal-declaration/

These groups brought the Living Earth/Earth Mother frame and language into the debates of Rio+20 as a counter to those who would put a price on Mother Earth and offer her up for sale. Communities across the United States are passing resolutions that affirm that nature has natural rights and that corporations do not.

Narrative 3: The Living Economy

The Living Economy narrative frames the culture and institutions of a new economy that works in co-productive partnership with nature to maintain the conditions essential to all life. It supports and enhances Earth's living systems. It provides livelihood opportunities for all people. It is radically democratic. And it advances Living Earth's evolutionary journey.

The Living Economy narrative is integral to the fast-growing New Economy movement. Business people speak of the responsibility of business to serve the common good. Investors speak of a living return that combines a modest financial return with the benefits of living in a healthy community with a healthy ecosystem. The homilies on economic justice of Pope Francis reach a vast audience with foundational moral truths. Multiracial leadership groups like Movement Generation are advancing a generative Earth frame among grassroots groups. Recent findings in science affirm that our health depends on our connection to nature and a caring community in which wealth is equitably distributed. We are learning that committing acts of kindness brings joy.

Thoughtful economists propose new indexes for economic performance that acknowledge the detrimental impacts of economic growth on people and nature. Local communities are coming together in national and global alliances like the American Independent Business Alliance, the Business Alliance for Local Living Economies, the New Economy Coalition, and Transition Towns to rebuild local economies based on locally owned socially and environmentally conscious businesses. Media outlets like *YES! Magazine* share the stories of possibility from such initiatives with an expanding global audience.

A widening public conversation melds these many insights into a grand synthesis story that reveals the inseparable interconnection of all being, the presence and creative power of distributed intelligent agency, and a profound cosmic purpose. The emerging story gives our human lives deep meaning, presents a compelling vision of human possibility, and invites our active participation in making that vision a reality.

All the while, the Sacred Money and Markets story continues to lose credibility. The Money Economy's corporate robots are far more vulnerable than they—or we—realize.

LET OUR VOICES RISE

Let us each find and share our version of a Sacred Life and Living Earth story and its joyful message of possibility.

- Begin with a personal reflection on the stories and cosmologies outlined in this book. Which story and

cosmology ring most true for you? How do you frame
the story that lives in your heart? What for you are
the personal implications? How might you bring the
language and framing of the new story and cosmology
into your normal daily conversations? See "Questions
for Reflection" at the end of this book.

- Invite friends and colleagues to read *Change the Story,
  Change the Future* and organize a conversation to share
  and explore their thoughts and reflections in search of a
  deeper, richer understanding for all. You will find a link
  on our *Change the Story, Change the Future* web page to
  a helpful discussion guide: http://livingeconomiesforum
  .org/ChangeTheStory-ChangeTheFuture.

- Organize a course or workshop in your church or
  university devoted to exploring the power of story and
  the many sources of understanding from which we may
  draw in framing a Living Universe cosmology consistent
  with the depth and breadth of human knowledge and an
  authentic sacred story adequate to the needs of our time.

- Join with those who are living the Sacred Life and
  Living Earth future. Find out what others are doing.
  Learn. Add your own energy and creativity. Countless
  initiatives are already under way. There is no one critical
  need or contribution. We are rebuilding everything—the
  economy, community, the built environment, education,
  law, science, and religion. Look around. Go with what
  best fits your gifts, passion, and relationships.

- As you live the Sacred Life and Living Earth story, tell
  the story in word as well as deed in your description and

explanation of what you are doing and in your invitation to others to join. Frame the reasoning behind your choice in the language and logic of the Sacred Life and Living Earth story.

- Insist that your opponents ground their arguments in the values and assumptions of the Sacred Life and Living Earth story.

- When assessing the economy's performance, choose metrics that reflect living-system health.

- Ask of every policy proposal: Does it serve life or money? Does it increase or decrease corporate monopoly control of the means of living? Does it favor the concentration or equitable distribution of ownership? Does it restore and enhance or further undermine the function of Earth's living systems? Does it strengthen relationships of caring and sharing or further monetize them?

- If you are involved in an organization advancing an environmental, peace, or justice agenda, engage your colleagues in addressing the following question: Does the organization's work ameliorate the consequences of a failed Sacred Money and Markets system (a homeless shelter)? Make adjustment at the margins of that system (demand penalties for banks that engage in illegal actions)? Or advance the turning to a new system that roots power in people and community and aligns with the values and assumptions of a Sacred Life and Living Earth story (establish cooperatively owned community-accountable financial institutions to finance and hold home mortgages)? Encourage the latter and use the Sacred Life and Living Earth story to frame the organization's message.

- In news reports, policy studies, and academic curricula listen for the underlying story. Does it reflect the values and assumptions of a Sacred Money and Markets story or a Sacred Life and Living Earth story? If the former, note and articulate in your mind the fallacies revealed when viewed through a Sacred Life and Living Earth lens. If appropriate, call out to others the fallacies introduced by a false and fabricated lens.

Share the story in your heart and spread its joyful message of possibility. Let us each find our favorite rendering among the story's rich variations. Invite others to join. Let our voices rise together as a mighty gospel choir, each voice with its place within the shifting harmonies and rhythms of the whole.

We will know we are on a path to a viable future when the corporate political flacks find themselves compelled to argue within our frame that their proposals will best serve life and heal our Living Earth mother.

OURS TO CHOOSE

Life is not a destination. It is a journey of exploration and discovery. We are born to contribute to that journey.

As far as we know, we humans are creation's most daring experiment in the evolutionary potential of reflective consciousness. Our history demonstrates the power of this potential for both good and ill.

In a mere two hundred thousand years—a mere blink of the eye in cosmic time—our species developed the capacity for speech, created complex languages, and mastered the use of fire. We learned to produce and use sophisticated tools, create great works of art, cultivate our own food, communicate in written form, establish organized systems of knowledge, and create great civilizations. We now reach out to the stars, plumb the inner secrets of matter and genetics, and strive to meld ourselves into an interconnected, inclusive, and deeply democratic global society.

Our positive progress provides living proof of the evolutionary potential of a species with the gift of reflective consciousness. Our experience also demonstrates the deadly risks when that gift is combined with partial knowledge and unbridled arrogance.

In a brief five-thousand-year fit of adolescent rebellion, we turned away from our Earth Mother to strike out on our own. As adolescents are sometimes wont to do, we put at grave risk our family and ourselves. We now face a defining test of our readiness to embrace the lessons of these troubled years.

Do we have the intelligence and good sense to return to our family, honor our Sacred Mother, and accept our adult responsibilities as Earth's most gifted and powerful species?

Let us embrace this moment as an opportunity to claim and express our true nature as living beings inhabiting a Living Earth in a Living Universe. Let us accept responsibility for our self-aware agency and learn the arts of living in a conscious interconnected world. And let us rethink and restructure our institutions to find our place of contribution to creation's continued unfolding.

We are far from a full understanding of our complex, vast, and wondrous universe. Yet our current understanding is sufficient to recognize that Earth is a living being and the only source of nurture we humans as a species are ever likely to have. We must accept and embrace the implications of this reality—and do so in a historical instant.

The fact that we humans seem naturally drawn to know, learn, and create is a source of hope for our common future. We need not know where creation's journey leads, or whether a final destination is even a meaningful concept. It is sufficient that we discern and celebrate its trajectory toward ever greater complexity, beauty, awareness, and possibility.

Our reward for our contribution is the inherent joy of living and the thrill of participating in life's quest to know, to reach beyond, and to become.

Our future is ours to choose. We are the ones we've been waiting for.

QUESTIONS FOR REFLECTION

After you read *Change the Future, Change the Story,* I encourage you to reflect on these questions. Then, invite selected friends to read the book and gather together to share reflections in search of a deeper understanding of the beliefs, stories, and possibilities that frame the human future.

1. THE SACRED MONEY AND MARKETS STORY

Are there significant ways in which the Sacred Money and Markets story affects your family and work life, your faith or spiritual life, the locality in which you live, or your politics? To what extent have you been inclined to passively accept it? Question it? Challenge it?

What main sources of influence have brought it into your life? How has your awareness of and response to it changed over time?

2. YOUR BELIEFS

Who and what initially informed, influenced, and helped shape your personal cosmology or beliefs about the nature of reality, your role in it, and your image or view of God or spirit? How have your beliefs evolved over the years? What learnings, observations, and experiences have had major shaping influences?

What is your earliest recollection of being in relationship with nature, and how has that relationship changed over time?

If *sacred* describes that which is most important, most worthy of our care and respect, and most essential to the well-being of humans and all life, what is most sacred to you?

3. A SACRED LIFE AND LIVING EARTH STORY

In what ways does the Sacred Life and Living Earth story ring true to you—or not? How does it align with or contrast with your views of science and religion? How is the new story reflected in your current personal choices? How might it further shape these choices?

4. CHANGING OUR SHARED STORY

What might be the specific implications for your life, your community, and global society if a Sacred Life and Living Earth story were to become our shared public story?

In what ways might you contribute to making that happen? Take a look at the suggestions in chapter 10 under the heading "Let Our Voices Rise."

Consider the organizations and groups in which you

have influence and reflect on how you might use everyday conversation to bring the frame and language of the Sacred Life and Living Earth story into the culture, programming, and public outreach of those organizations and groups.

To engage a group in a deeper conversation about *Change the Future, Change the Story,* find the link to a helpful Discussion Guide at http://livingeconomiesforum.org/ ChangeTheStory-ChangeTheFuture.

N O T E S

Prologue

1. For a report on our conclusions from this ten-day reflection, see Asian NGO Coalition, NGOC, IRED Asia, and the PCDForum, "Economy, Ecology & Spirituality: A Theory and Practice of Sustainability," *Living Economies Forum*, n.d., http://living economiesforum.org/economy-ecology-spirituality.

2. Marcus J. Borg, *The God We Never Knew: Beyond Dogmatic Religion to a More Authentic Contemporary Faith* (New York: HarperCollins, 1997), chap. 3, "Imaging God: Why and How It Matters."

3. David Korten, "A Plea for Rio+20: Don't Commodify Nature," *Yes! Blogs,* April 24, 2012, http://www.yesmagazine.org/blogs/ david-korten/a-plea-for-rio-20-dont-commodify-nature (http://bit .ly/1tvpLJ6).

4. David Korten, "A New Story for a New Economy," March 5, 2014, http://www.yesmagazine.org/pdf/kortennewstory.pdf.

Chapter 1

1. This process was no accident. In *The Crash of 2016* (New York: Twelve, 2013) Thom Hartmann documents the history of efforts of

wealthy oligarchs to make the United States a plutocracy, giving particular attention to the most recent three decades.

2. Donella H. Meadows, Dennis L. Meadows, Jørgen Randers, and William W. Behrens III, *The Limits to Growth: A Report for the Club of Rome's Project on the Predicament of Mankind* (New York: Universe Books), 1972.

3. For an overview of the assessment of the vulnerability of the existing system by Robert David Steele, a former high-level U.S. intelligence community insider, see Nafeez Ahmen, "The Open Source Revolution Is Coming and It Will Conquer the 1%—ex CIA Spy," *Earth Insight* (blog), in *The Guardian*, June 19, 2014, http://www.theguardian.com/environment/earth-insight/2014/jun/19/open-source-revolution-conquer-one-percent-cia-spy (http://bit.ly/1nnuu8U).

4. Philip Low, "The Cambridge Declaration on Consciousness," ed. Jaak Panksepp et al., July 7, 2012, http://fcmconference.org/img/CambridgeDeclarationOnConsciousness.pdf.

Chapter 2

1. Kurt Johnson and David Robert Ord, *The Coming Interspiritual Age* (Vancouver, BC: Namaste Publishing, 2012), 206.

2. "Do the Best You Can but Don't Expect to Win," interview with Ajarn Sulak Sivaraksa, in *Ecological Buddhism,* n.d., http://www.ecobuddhism.org/wisdom/interviews/ajss/.

Chapter 3

1. Stuart A. Kauffman, *Reinventing the Sacred: A New View of Science, Reason, and Religion* (New York: Basic Books, 2008), 19–30.

2. "The Blind Men and the Elephant," a poem by John Godfrey Saxe (1816–1887), posted in Duen Hsi Yen, *Noogenesis* (blog), last

updated 2 February 2008, http://www.noogenesis.com/pineapple/
blind_men_elephant.html.

3. Richard Panek, *The 4% Universe: Dark Matter, Dark Energy,
and the Race to Discover the Rest of Reality* (New York: Houghton
Mifflin, 2011).

4. Gina Kolata, "In Good Health? Thank Your 100 Trillion
Bacteria," *New York Times*, June 13, 2012, http://nyti.ms/M3Hq1p.

5. The label "Living Universe" comes from the book of that
name by my longtime friend and colleague Duane Elgin, *The Living
Universe* (San Francisco: Berrett-Koehler Publishers, 2009).

Chapter 4

1. *Overview*, a short film on the life-altering experience of the
astronauts who viewed Earth from space. Presented by Planetary
Collective, http://vimeo.com/55073825.

2. Brian Thomas Swimme and Mary Evelyn Tucker, *Journey of
the Universe* (New Haven, CT: Yale University Press, 2011). See also
the Swimme and Tucker documentary film *Journey of the Universe:
An Epic Story of Cosmic, Earth, and Human Transformation*,
and Brian Swimme and Thomas Berry, *The Universe Story:
From the Primordial Flaring Forth to the Ecozoic Era* (New York:
HarperCollins Publishers, 1992).

3. See David Suzuki with Amanda McConnell and Adrienne
Mason, *The Sacred Balance: Rediscovering Our Place in Nature*
(Vancouver, BC: Greystone Books, 2007) for a richly detailed
account of the diverse and intricate complexity of Earth's organisms
and the self-directing living systems by which they create and
maintain the conditions of their own existence.

4. Malcolm Hollick, *The Science of Oneness: A Worldview for the
Twenty-First Century* (O Books: Hants, UK, 2006), 163–164.

5. Nicholas Wade, "Your Body Is Younger Than You Think," *New*

York Times, August 2, 2005, http://www.nytimes.com/2005/08/02/science/02cell.html.

6. Melissa K. Nelson, ed., *Original Instructions* (Rochester, VT: Bear & Company, 2008).

7. Matthew D. Lieberman, *Social: Why Our Brains Are Wired to Connect* (New York: Crown Publishers, 2013); and Colin Tudge, *Why Genes Are Not Selfish and People Are Nice* (Edinburgh, UK: Floris Books, 2013).

8. Mae-Wan Ho, *The Rainbow and the Worm: The Physics of Organisms,* 3rd ed. (Singapore: World Scientific Publishing, 2008).

9. Richard Wilkinson and Kate Pickett, *The Spirit Level: Why More Equal Societies Almost Always Do Better* (London: Penguin Books, 2009).

Chapter 5

1. Dennis Overbye, "Far-Off Planets Like the Earth Dot the Galaxy," *New York Times,* November 4, 2013, http://nyti.ms/WfEJVk.

2. Lynn Margulis and Dorion Sagan, "Marvellous Microbes," *Resurgence & Ecologist,* no. 206, May–June 2001. See also Margulis and Sagan, *What Is Life?* (New York: Simon & Schuster, 1995); and Sidney Liebes, Elisabet Sahtouris, and Brian Swimme, *A Walk through Time: From Stardust to Us: The Evolution of Life on Earth* (New York: John Wiley, 1998).

3. Peter A. Corning, *Holistic Darwinism: Synergy, Cybernetics, and the Bioeconomics of Evolution* (Chicago: University of Chicago Press, 2005); David Sloan Wilson, *Evolution for Everyone: How Darwin's Theory Can Change the Way We Think about Our Lives* (New York: Bantam Dell, 2007).

4. Thomas Berry, "The Exozoic Era," 11th annual E. F.

Schumacher Lecture, October 1991, Schumacher Center for a New Economics, http://www.centerforneweconomics.org/publications/lectures/berry/thomas/the-ecozoic-era.

Chapter 7

1. This history is developed in greater detail in David C. Korten, *The Great Turning: From Empire to Earth Community* (San Francisco: Berrett-Koehler Publishers, 2006), Part II: Sorrows of Empire.

2. Marjorie Kelly, *The Divine Right of Capital* (San Francisco: Berrett-Koehler Publishers, 2001).

3. Robert L. Nadeau, *Rebirth of the Sacred: Science, Religion, and the New Environmental Ethos* (New York: Oxford University Press, 2013).

Chapter 8

1. The implications as Roxas outlined them are obvious, profound, and ignored by most economists. He subsequently spelled out the significance of the distinction in two papers posted on the Living Economies Forum website. They are even more relevant today than they were when he wrote them in 1991. See Sixto Roxas, "The Ideological Roots of Crisis in an Archipelagic Country," October 4, 1991, http://livingeconomiesforum.org/1991/CRISIS, and "Community-Centered Capitalism: An NGO Alternative," December 1, 1991, http://livingeconomiesforum.org/1991/22roxas.

2. For more elaboration on the distinction between real wealth and phantom wealth, see David C. Korten, *Agenda for a New Economy: From Phantom Wealth to Real Wealth*, 2nd ed. (San Francisco: Berrett-Koehler Publishers, 2010).

Chapter 9

1. I recommend the powerful video documentary *The House I Live In,* http://www.thehouseilivein.org/.

2. Marjorie Kelly, *Owning Our Future: The Emerging Ownership Revolution* (San Francisco: Berrett-Koehler Publishers, 2012).

3. Gar Alperovitz, *America beyond Capitalism: Reclaiming Our Wealth, Our Liberty, and Our Democracy* (Hoboken, NJ: Wiley, 2005), chap. 7, "A Direct Stake in Economic Life: Worker-Owned Firms." Marjorie Kelly and Shanna Ratner, "A Different Kind of Ownership Society," *YES! Magazine,* August 3, 2010, http://www .yesmagazine.org/new-economy/a-different-kind-of-ownership-society. See also *Shift Change,* a video documentary by Mark Dworkin and Melissa Young, http://shiftchange.org/.

4. The argument and structure of the proposed system, including the appropriate role of the Federal Reserve, are spelled out in David Korten, *How to Liberate America from Wall Street Rule,* The New Economy Working Group, July 2011, http://www.neweconomywork inggroup.org/new-economy-story/how-liberate-america-wall-street-rule (http://bit.ly/1CsUB7P).

Chapter 10

1. You can find a great many such stories on the *YES! Magazine* website, http://www.yesmagazine.org/.

2. David Korten, "We Know Who Stole the Economy—National People's Action Moves to Take It Back," *YES! Magazine,* December 3, 2013, http://www.yesmagazine.org/new-economy/we-know-who-stole-the-economy-national-people2019s-action-moves-to-take-it-back (http://bit.ly/1bPybmd).

ACKNOWLEDGMENTS

I've written this book in the style of an essay to summarize the accumulated learning and insights of 77 years of unusually varied experiences.

Many thousands of sources and individuals have shaped the thoughts I share here. I have acknowledged only a very few in the text and references. I extend thanks and my apology to those left unmentioned. I make no claim that any idea in this volume is original with me. I find it a remarkable source of hope that so many people quickly find most of the thoughts presented here to be self-evident.

My contribution is to affirm self-evident truths often ignored or denied in public discourse. To weave the elements together in ways that may help readers make critical connections previously unnoted. And to provide language that readers may find useful in sharing the resulting understanding with others.

Many people and organizations made distinctive contributions essential to this book.

Thanks to Jeff Campbell of the Christensen Fund and Tom Kruse of the Rockefeller Brothers Fund, who organized, and invited me to participate in, the March 2012 Green Economy retreat at the Pocantico Retreat Center. This experience awakened me to the significance to the future of humanity of the indigenous belief that Earth is our sacred living mother. And to Karma Tshiteem, head of the Bhutan Gross National Happiness Commission, who awakened with a powerful emotional energy a truth buried deep in my being when he spoke three words: *Time is life.*

My thanks to Ian Johnson and Karl Wagner of the Club of Rome for including me in a June 2012 values discussion meeting in Bristol, England that launched the organization's ValuesQuest initiative. That discussion inspired me to draft the original reflection piece that evolved over two and a half years to become this book. I am especially indebted to Anders Wijkman and Ernst Ulrich von Weizsäcker, co-presidents of the Club of Rome, who organized the acceptance of this book as a report to the Club of Rome and provided the foreword. This has a very special personal meaning for me. The original report to the Club of Rome, *The Limits to Growth*, was my initial introduction to a global-system perspective. I was at the time in awe of the book's global impact and the moral and intellectual power of the organization that brought it to world attention.

I owe a special debt to Dena Merriam and the Contemplative Alliance for organizing two conferences exploring the themes of my initial exploratory essay. These conferences inspired new insights and deepened my sense of the importance of delving yet deeper into our framing cosmologies.

I also want to thank my colleagues on the board and staff of YES! Magazine, who have made an invaluable contribution to framing the New Economy/Living Economy vision and to making it a unifying frame for the many organizations and individuals working to create a world that works for all. YES! Magazine is the go-to communications organization for news of the New Economy. Special credit goes to editor-in-chief Sarah van Gelder, who shaped and holds YES! Magazine's editorial vision.

My colleagues who form the core of the virtual New Economy think tank organized under the banner New Economy Working Group bear special mention and appreciation. An informal alliance of the Institute for Policy Studies (IPS), YES! Magazine, the Living Economies Forum, the Democracy Collaborative, the New Economy Coalition, and the Institute for Local Self-Reliance—coordinated by IPS and Noel Ortega—it serves as an ongoing source of ideas, inspiration, and critical review. Gar Alperovitz, Sarah Anderson, John Cavanagh, Fran Korten, Gus Speth, and Sarah van Gelder deserve special mention.

And thanks go to members of the board of my institutional home base, the Living Economies Forum: Puanani Burgess, Frances Moore Lappé, Harry Pickens, and Roberto Vargas. Special thanks to Kat Gjovik, the Living Economies Forum director of communications and outreach, who provided essential feedback on every draft.

Very special thanks to my wife and life partner, Fran Korten, the executive director of YES! Magazine, who has provided inspiration and insight at every step along the way.

Thanks to Steve Piersanti and all the staff at Berrett-Koehler Publishers who have provided me with exceptional professional editorial, design, and marketing support for each of my trade books—beginning with *When Corporations Rule the World*. It is an extraordinary experience as an author to have the total backing of an extraordinarily talented professional publishing team committed to doing everything in their ability to help me communicate my message clearly and effectively to the widest possible audience. In addition, a special thanks to Jeevan Sivasubramaniam of the B-K staff for suggesting that an essay I shared with him be expanded into this book, to Charlotte Ashlock for her contribution to disciplining my writing, and to Karen Seriguchi for her support and contribution as the ultimate copyeditor.

I also want to mention a few of the many other friends and colleagues who have offered specific suggestions and feedback at various stages during the writing of this book and the two essays on which it is based. They include Barry Andrews, Tom Atlee, Ed Bacon, Diane Berke, Shannon Biggs, Anna Elza Brady, Ravi Chaudhry, Joan Chittister, David Christopher, Peter Corning, Gopal Dayaneni, Tracy Loeffelholz Dunn, Duane Elgin, Rob Ellman, Ted Falcon, Matthew Fox, Tim Fox, Lorna Garano, Marybeth Gardam, Rob Garrity, Matthew Gilbert, Gary Gripp, Thom Hartmann, Christa Hillstrom, Charles Holmes, Garry Jacobs, Kurt Johnson, Ellyn Kerr, Brian McLaren, Jason McLennan, Annie Leonard, Don Mackenzie, Bob Massie, Graeme Maxton, Robert Nadeau, Winston Negan, Mateo Nube, Rebecca Nyamidie, Martin Palmer, Barry Peters, Bill Phipps, Doug Pibel, Jamal Rahman, Steven Rockefeller, Gideon Rosenblatt, Marthine Satris, Otto Scharmer, Bob Scott, Lucianne Siers, Ralph Singh, Brian Swimme, Michael Townsend, Lama Tsomo, Mary Evelyn Tucker, Bill Twist, and Richard Wilson, among others.

INDEX

ABOUT THE AUTHOR

DR. DAVID C. KORTEN worked for more than thirty-five years in preeminent business, academic, and international development institutions before he turned away from the establishment to become a leading critic of what he now calls the Money Economy and a proponent of a Living Economy based on living-system design principles.

He is the co-founder and board chair of *YES! Magazine*, a co-chair of the New Economy Working Group, the president of the Living Economies Forum, an associate fellow of the Institute for Policy Studies, a member of the Club of Rome, a founding board member emeritus of the Business Alliance for Local Living Economies, and a former founding associate of the International Forum on Globalization. He earned MBA and PhD degrees from the Stanford University Graduate School of Business and served on the faculty of the Harvard Business School.

Trained in psychology, organization theory, business

strategy, and economics, he devoted his early career to advancing business education in low-income countries. With his wife, Fran Korten, he set up the College of Business Administration in the Haile Selassie I University in Ethiopia, while completing his doctoral studies at the Stanford Business School. He completed his military service during the Vietnam War as a captain in the US Air Force, with duty at the Special Air Warfare School, Air Force headquarters command, the Office of the Secretary of Defense, and the Advanced Research Projects Agency.

He served as the Harvard Business School adviser to the Central American Management Institute in Nicaragua and headed a Harvard Institute for International Development project to strengthen the organization and management of national family planning programs funded by the Ford Foundation.

In the late 1970s, Korten left US academia and moved to Southeast Asia, where he lived for nearly fifteen years, serving first as a Ford Foundation project specialist and later as Asia regional adviser on development management to the US Agency for International Development.

In 1988, he walked away from the establishment to work with leading Asian nongovernmental organizations on identifying the root causes of development failure in the region and building the capacity of civil society organizations everywhere to function as strategic catalysts of positive national and global change. He and his colleagues concluded that the root cause of development failure resides in economic models and policies promoted by the United States to advance the consolidation of global corporate rule.

In 1990 he founded the People-Centered Development Forum, now the Living Economies Forum, to engage with colleagues in exposing the failures of established economic models and defining alternatives.

In 1992, he and Fran returned to the United States to share with their fellow Americans the lessons of their years abroad. They settled in a New York apartment near Union Square between Madison Avenue and Wall Street, where he wrote *When Corporations Rule the World*. It launched in 1995 and became an international bestseller. In 1994 he participated in the formation of the International Forum on Globalization and in 1995–96 in the founding of YES! Magazine.

In 1998, he and Fran moved to Bainbridge Island, where Fran became executive director of YES! Magazine and David wrote in succession *The Post-Corporate World: Life after Capitalism*; *The Great Turning: From Empire to Earth Community*; and *Agenda for a New Economy: From Phantom Wealth to Real Wealth*. In 2001 he participated in founding the Business Alliance for Local Living Economies and in 2008 the New Economy Working Group.

DAVID KORTEN

http://livingeconomiesforum.org
https://facebook.com/davidkorten
Twitter: @dkorten

Subscribe to YES! Magazine

Each issue of
YES! Magazine delivers
powerful ideas and
practical actions.
Ad free.

Follow us

Facebook:
/yesmagazine

Twitter:
@yesmagazine

Online at:
yesmagazine.org

Get the Best of YES! each week

Readers tell us our
email newsletter raises their
spirits and enlivens their
imagination for building a
better world.

Also by David Korten

Agenda for a New Economy
From Phantom Wealth to Real Wealth, 2nd Edition

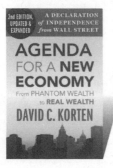

The Wall Street economy has perfected the art of creating "phantom wealth" financial assets without producing anything of real value. Periodic, devastating crashes will continue until it is replaced by a New Economy of locally based, community-oriented, living enterprises that create real wealth in service to people, community, and nature. Korten explains why this is so and provides in-depth advice on how we can bring it about.

Paperback, 336 pages, ISBN 978-1-60509-375-8
PDF ebook, ISBN 978-1-60509-376-5

The Great Turning
From Empire to Earth Community

David Korten exposes the destructive and oppressive nature of "Empire," the organization of society through hierarchy and violence that has held sway since ancient times. Drawing on evolutionary theory, developmental psychology, religious teachings, and other sources, Korten shows that "Earth Community"—an egalitarian, sustainable way of ordering human society—is indeed possible, and he lays out a grassroots strategy for achieving it.

Paperback, 424 pages, ISBN 978-1-887208-08-6
PDF ebook, ISBN 978-1-57675-539-6

BK Berrett–Koehler Publishers, Inc.
www.bkconnection.com   **800.929.2929**

When Corporations Rule the World

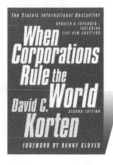

In this modern classic, called "a searing indictment of an unjust international economic order" by Archbishop Desmond Tutu, David Korten details the threat economic globalization poses to long-term human interests and outlines a strategy for empowering local communities to resist corporate power.

"This book will agitate your mind, elevate your soul, and engage your civic spirit."
—**Ralph Nader**

Paperback, 400 pages, ISBN 978-1-887208-04-8

The Post-Corporate World
Life after Capitalism

There is a deep chasm between the promises of the new global capitalism and the reality of social breakdown, spiritual emptiness, and environmental destruction it is leaving in its wake. Korten outlines an alternative: a global system of thriving, healthy market economies that organize by living system principles and function as extensions of healthy local ecosystems to meet the livelihood needs of all people and communities.

Paperback, 336 pages, ISBN 978-1-887208-03-1
PDF ebook, ISBN 978-1-60509-396-3

BK Berrett–Koehler Publishers, Inc.
www.bkconnection.com   **800.929.2929**